50 Real Gho

Terrifying real life encounters

By MJ Wayland

"It is, alas, chiefly the evil emotions that are able to leave their photographs on surrounding scenes and objects and whoever heard of a place haunted by a noble deed, or of beautiful and lovely ghosts revisiting the glimpses of the moon?"

Algernon H. Blackwood

Paperback published 1st March 2013

Copyright © 2013 MJ Wayland

978-1-909667-00-6

Published by Hob Hill Books
www.hobhill.com

Author website
www.mjwayland.com

CONTENTS

FOREWORD

A ghost story should never end perfectly. That is my rule of thumb. After investigating ghost experiences for nearly thirty years, I realised that the finely polished stories told by storytellers and "ghost walkers" were exactly that – polished. In polishing stories we lose the personality of the haunted and indeed the haunter itself, that's why in my books, research papers and articles, I always maintain the original testaments and facts.

The stories that I have collected for you now are rough diamonds, totally unpolished and any additions by myself are kept to a minimum and noted clearly. This book is a collection of some of the most strangest, weirdest and down right spookiest stories I have uncovered over the last three decades.

As I began to compile these stories I began to realise that I was actually becoming very affected by them and I am sure you will too. There is no doubt you will have your favourites once you have read the book, but mine are as follows. One of the standout stories for me, is "Ghost with no mouth" – a series of terrifying experiences in a modern house in which the witness's child describes the ghost as having "no mouth and wears black boots but is naughty". The experiences were very real to the family involved, and you wonder if "Black Square" continues to haunt this dwelling.

Another story "The Mystery Lady" is downright creepy, a man encounters a strange woman on a deserted train station, she mumbles to herself and refuses to get onboard the last train to Portsmouth. The next day he discovers that he was actually talking to a ghost! I spare you the details so not to spoil the story, but you will certainly have a chill!

In total there are fifty real experiences with ghosts and spirits included in this book and all direct from the witnesses themselves. None of them wanted their names publishing or any publicity about their experiences but all of them had the need to share, and share they have done.

MJ Wayland
June 2012

EXPERIENCES IN AN OLD LONDON PUB

The Queen's Larder pub is fascinating, taking it's name from Queen Charlotte, wife of the 'Mad King' George III, who was receiving treatment for his apparent insanity at a doctors house in the square where it is situated. The Queen assisted in the nursing of her husband, by cooking for him and rented a small cellar beneath the pub, where she kept special foods for him. With the area having such a long and esteemed history there is no doubt that some of its previous inhabitants still wander.

"I once used to run the Queens Larder pub in Queen Square, London, WC1. There was many experiences reported by staff and customers and over the years we realised that one ghost was more frequent than the others. Eventually we established that her name was Mary Wells.

She had been falsely accused of a crime and hidden in the attic of the pub but was eventually found and hanged. I have lots of stories to tell about her activities, which were never malicious, but seemed more about her wanting to tell her story. I have never researched to see if anyone by that name was in fact hanged so have not been able to verify what actually happened. However, the experiences were real and witnessed by many of my family and staff.

While at the Queens Larder I was 'visited' by the spirit of my ex-husband, whom to my knowledge at that time was still alive, but I hadn't seen or heard from him in around ten years. I was convinced that I was hallucinating as I had his two sons and felt sure that his family would have contacted me to let the boys know if anything was wrong. He visited me many times and told me several things. I later found out (through an old friend who had spent five years trying to find me) that he had died around the time I first had the visitation.

I have had many experiences and encounters but none have been terrifying and have been very rewarding."

MY CHILD'S GHOST

About six years ago I moved into a maisonette which had just been purchased by my parents. I had been in the place for a couple of months and everything was fine. One night I put my two year old daughter to bed, all was quiet for a while so I did the usual and went upstairs to check on her. She was sound asleep in her cot but as I walked out of the room and onto the landing, I felt a breeze rush past me. It felt like someone had walked passed me and there was a very strong smell of lavender.

I went downstairs putting it down to my imagination. About five minutes later, I heard my daughter start talking so I went upstairs and turned on the bedroom light. I asked my daughter who she was talking to and she pointed to something across the room and she said she was talking to the lady.

This happened on several occasions and sometimes in the middle of the night I would hear my daughter talking and laughing with someone. Some mornings I would go into her bedroom and she would have glitter on her face.

Around this time, a friend of mine came to visit one afternoon. When she left, she put some cigarettes on the coffee table as I had run out of them. I walked her to her car and went back inside. I remember noticing the cigarettes on the table and I went upstairs to the toilet. On my return, the cigarettes were nowhere to be seen. There was no one else in the house at the time, my partner was still at work and my daughter was at my parent's house. I looked under the coffee table and saw that the rug underneath had been rolled up into a tube. I unravelled it to find the cigarettes inside. Obviously my bad habits were not appreciated!

Another time, myself and my partner had just gone up to bed, our daughter was asleep and our cat was curled up at

9

the end of the bed. Suddenly I heard the phone start to beep as though it had been left off the hook. My partner went downstairs to find that this is what had happened but none of us had used the phone that night. Also it was one of those phones that was attached to the wall so it couldn't have been knocked off the hook rather it would have had to have been lifted.

If I stood at the top of my stairs, I would always get a feeling of someone rushing up the stairs past me and out of the corner of my eye I would see a figure but if I looked directly at it, it was never there. This went on for the first year that we lived in the maisonette. Things calmed down and for a while nothing really happened.

Then we encountered a run of bad luck. I had seven miscarriages including losing a baby when I was five months pregnant and I also lost my Grandmother who I was very close to.

Finally last year I gave birth to a beautiful baby girl after having an extremely difficult and worrying pregnancy. I spent the last two months of my pregnancy in bed unable to walk. I remember one particularly hot summers day, I was in bed, my partner at work and my daughter at school. I burst into tears as I was so fed up. I have to point out that we had swapped bedrooms with my daughter.

Anyway, I noticed in the corner of the room some lights had started to appear. For the first time in five years I smelt the lavender scent and I began to hear a female voice. Although I didn't hear the voice physically, it was definitely in my head. It was a voice of a lady reassuring me that everything was fine and it would all be over soon.

At the time I was thirty five weeks pregnant. The next week I gave birth to my daughter. She was four weeks premature but as strong as an ox!

A couple of weeks later, I woke up one night and again in the same corner of the room the lights appeared. I then noticed a very tall figure bending over my baby daughter's crib. I had the feeling that the figure was smiling at her and meant her no harm. I also had the feeling that who ever this person was, they were very pleased that we finally had a healthy baby.

I know that a few of my neighbours had also had strange experiences in their homes.

A neighbour of mine had a startling experience one night. She was rushed at by a dark shadow. Another neighbour had things moved a lot and heard scratching sounds in her bedroom. Another had watched a kitchen knife lift off of the kitchen worktop and travel across the room before dropping to the floor. Several friends of hers witnessed this.

I was intrigued by my haunting so I decided to investigate myself. I knew a lady I wouldn't call her a friend more of an associate who claimed to be a medium. I never mentioned anything to her about what had been going on in my home and none of my friends or relatives knew her so no one could have said anything before her visit.

As soon as she arrived, she commented on the smell of lavender and she then said she felt a presence of a young lady who had lived in the maisonette years ago (the maisonettes were built in the 50s). My friend said she had the feeling that the young lady was running away from something or somebody and that she had stayed in the maisonette because she had felt safe.

We moved out of there a few months ago and bought our own house, but we go back to the maisonette regularly as my parents own the place and are redecorating to let it out to the next tenant. On a recent visit, my partner went up into the loft to clear out all of our Christmas decorations, old toys, baby clothes etc. Whilst he was up there he found some old paintings which neither of us remember being up there before. He bought them down and on closer inspection they had been painted by a girl called Laura. Unfortunately, there was no date on them but it is a mystery how they got there.

Like I said before, we go back quite often and I always feel like I'm being welcomed. One night as I sat in the car as we were leaving, I looked up at our old block and I swear I saw a figure standing at the window of our old bedroom watching us leave.

THE RUSSIAN GHOST

I saw a ghost while I was away on holiday in Russia. I was travelling by coach in a party of eight to twelve others. We had been travelling most of the day to get to the town of Kostrumo, in the Golden ring outside of Moscow. The countryside consists of vast expanses of Siberian Silver Birch and forests. As we neared the village I noticed out of the window on my left a graveyard. Standing next to a grave was what I assumed to be a woman in a black cloak, who was a widow, mourning the loss of her husband. It was strange, but not unusual to see this.

I noticed that in the graveyard was an orchard of cherry trees. I did not think too much about this and looked away. I then took a glance again over my shoulder. As I looked back through the coach window, the figure had moved and was now standing next to a low wall and the wrought iron gates, the main entrance. The figure was ominously tall, looking much more than normal, and took on a threatening presence or shape. I noticed that there was no face in the hood of the cloaked figure. Far more disturbing, though, was that it seemed to be watching me and its hands were rested upon the top wall. I got a glimpse of its hands - it was not human! The hands and fingers on them were very long - over a meter in length and were skeletal, long and bony.

As I continued to look back at it, a skull appeared in the hood and two orange eyes looked back and it grinned at me. I looked away instantly and did not look back, as I figured that it represented death. I thought I must have been imagining things, so I tried to put the whole thing out of my mind and get on with the rest of the holiday.

One thing that did strike me as odd was that the graveyard was completely run down and overgrown with long grass; no one had been there in months or, in fact, years. So what was this figure doing there? I did not think too much about the incident and had forgotten about it.

Two days later, I arrived at a new hotel and had sat down to eat dinner in the main restaurant along with other Japanese guests.   As I ate, I looked up into the corner of the restaurant, and it was decorated with pots and other antiques.   But what drew my attention was a large wood carving by a Russian artist of a figure from Russian folklore. My blood chilled to the bone. For there was a carving of a hooded figure - a man who looked like a monk. His eyes were black looking and the arms on the figure were completely outstretched, its fingers were long and bony, at least over a metre long. This was exactly what I had seen in the graveyard. I knew then that what I had seen was indeed real.

VANISHING SCHOOLGIRL

I attended a small English boarding school located in the leafy suburbs approximately thirty miles from London.

The school building was a modest mansion (previously a family home) whose entire upstairs had been converted into the boarders' dormitories. Thanks to the Victorian architecture these could only be accessed by following lots of narrow twisting corridors, small landings and stairs that branched off almost randomly.

This incident occurred when I was fourteen and was boarding in the top-floor dormitory. One day at morning break I realised I'd left my Maths textbook on my bed so I raced upstairs to get it before the bell rang.

I ran up the main flight of stairs, through a fire door and past the Matron's office. The dorms were deserted because everyone was in class, but at this point I was joined by another girl, running just ahead of me so I couldn't see her face. She was blonde, wearing the school uniform (at the time we had a particularly fetching brown bri-nylon design which was hard to miss) and a purple scrunchy in her hair.

So we were running up to the dorms together, round corners, down corridors, through fire doors (being ahead of me, she would go first and I would catch the door on its back swing) and so on. As we got closer to the top dorm I began to wonder who she was because from the back she didn't resemble anyone in my year. All this took place in a matter of two minutes though, you understand, so it was just an idle thought.

Finally we got to the top landing - she was making for my dorm and definitely wasn't in my year so I was about to say something, when she pushed open the dorm door, ran in, I followed directly after her and...

... Arrived in an empty room.

I was completely and utterly alone. I remember very clearly the feeling of total brain freeze as I took in the fact that the girl had disappeared. It was a sunny autumn day and I could see motes of dust moving undisturbed in shafts of light from the window.

After about three minutes of just standing still in shock I half-heartedly poked under beds and in cupboards, but I knew it was hopeless. There wasn't anywhere she could have closeted herself in as I'd been less than a foot behind her when entering the room.

In the end I just grabbed my textbook and made my way back to class. I didn't tell anyone what happened for many years afterwards and I am still not sure I believe in ghosts.

THE GLASGOW GHOST

In the early 1970s in Glasgow, Scotland, my Grand-father Willie who was an agent for various pop groups was left alone in his house for the first time since he moved in. His wife had gone out to one of her singing gigs along with their young daughter, he had not been drinking and has never taken drugs, neither was he on any medication at that time.

At around 2:00am in the morning he went to visit the lavatory and then obviously came back to bed. He was lying awake when he heard heavy breathing beside him. He thought that it must be his own breathing but when he held his breath the 'other breathing' continued. He then almost immediately felt a huge heavy weight on his chest and really thought he was going to die of suffocation. He said over and over in his mind, "God, help me, God, help me". The pressure eased almost immediately even though this incantation was silent.

Willie said he rushed out of the bedroom and into the living room where he said that he looked into a mirror and saw his hair standing on end. He rushed out of the house and drove around until it was light.

When he recounted the story to his wife, it frightened her enough for them to put their double mattress in the living room for over six months before they could sell the house. However, during that time, he said that his body sweated out a real stink for quite a few weeks after this incident and he has never been able to explain any of it.
We still can't work out what happened to Willie, and even when he recalls it today you can see the fear in him.

THE GHOST OF ST ALBANS

I live in the old market town of St Albans in South East England. Our town was built by the Romans and we have a fourteenth century abbey and streets close to the modern city centre. All in all, a very beautiful and ancient place to live.

One day my mother happened to mention over lunch that our dog had refused to walk past a house in the medieval village of St. Michaels. I didn't believe her at all, so took him down there myself.

To my astonishment when we got to number sixty one or so, he stopped dead and put his claws into the ground and wouldn't move - sounds a bit cruel but I needed to be convinced. He did this every single time we walked past but was fine again literally two steps further down the road, once we picked him up and carried him forward. We watched the actions of other dogs but no other ever had the same fear.

We discovered that the house had often been bought and sold. There seemed to always be a 'for sale' sign outside. Anyway reading through some history of the place, we found out that there were tunnels under all of these houses that the monks used to use to go to the abbey nearby. Not scary at all really, but further investigation told us that this particular house was built on the site of an old abattoir. I cannot believe though that a dog could smell blood that was a few hundred years old - if that indeed was the case! We'll never know.

THE HOTEL MYSTERY

On the 26th February 2004 my sister Claire, who lives in Malin Bridge, Sheffield, locked her house up and headed off to bed. It was 10:00pm, her husband John and two children, Charlie, thirteen years old and Louise, ten years old were already in bed.

She made her way to the toilet, which stands separate from the bathroom in a long corridor style room with the toilet at the end of it. There was absolutely nothing on the floor and the window was tight shut.

The next morning at 6:30am she got up and went to the toilet, there on the floor was a folded A4 cream piece of paper. On further inspection she discovered it was an invoice for a well-known hotel in Scarborough, North Yorkshire. It was invoiced to a Mr Simons with a Charnock address near Gleadless, Sheffield. It was for one night stay on the 6th December 2003 and had a pink visa card receipt stapled to the top left hand corner of the page.

She asked her husband if he knew anything about it and also her children, none of them had seen it before or had heard of a Mr Simons. What was more astonishing was that the invoice was not in an addressed envelope and was in pristine condition as if it had just come straight off the printer.

Almost a week later on the 3rd March 2004, I called round her house to collect a letter I had been expecting. I noticed the cream paper underneath my letter and asked (being nosey) what it was. She asked me to see if I recognised the name or the address, which I didn't. She told me how it had appeared between the hours of 10:00pm Thursday night and 6:30am Friday morning and that nobody had a clue how it got there.

I asked her why she still had it and had she looked into it at all, to which she replied "No, I've been meaning to throw it away about four times this week but every time I had this thought, something made me put it back on top of the television."

I decided I would investigate for her so the next day I took the invoice to work and got the telephone number of Mr Simons from directory of enquiries and phoned it up. I finally came into contact with a Mr Simons who had no knowledge of a hotel in Scarborough let alone the invoice. He suggested it might be his son who travels round the country with his job, and said he would ask him to phone me when he got in from work.

Later that night I had a call from Mr Simons junior saying that everything was correct, he did stay in that hotel and that was his credit card number. He also remembered the invoice was folded into three with a visa slip staple to the top left hand corner. I asked him several questions to see if he knew anyone in my sister's family or even my family? I asked him if he had received the invoice by post, he said he had been given the invoice in the hotel as he checked out on the Sunday and he personally folded it into three then put it in the glove compartment of his car. When he got home he took it in the house with him and up to his bedroom.

About a month ago he decided to throw it away, he placed it in his bin in his bedroom without screwing it up. I asked him "what happened to the rubbish?" He said his mother would have emptied his bin into the main wheelie bin outside. We tried to think of any logical explanations of how it could have got into a locked house in the middle of the night in pristine condition from the other end of Sheffield, where it had been thrown away a month earlier. Even if someone had taken it out of his wheelie bin it would have been crumpled and dog-eared by the time it reached my sisters.

I decided to invite him over to the house to meet us all in the hope that something might fall into place. On Friday 5th March he arrived at the house but none of us recognised him. He wasn't even in my sister or my age bracket - I'm thirty eight and my sister Claire is forty, where as Mr (Adam) Simons Junior is twenty one years of age. The only slight link we uncovered was that he was studying at Sheffield Hallam University doing a Property Management and Surveying course and Claire is also at Sheffield Hallam doing a Housing Management course. We discovered that their paths could not have crossed because Adam finished last August to do a sandwich year and Claire didn't start until September.

He told us that he had taken a (now ex-) girlfriend with him to the hotel. He asked Claire if she knew her as she was also at university doing a module but Claire had no knowledge of this name at all.

I asked Adam if he had ever had a paranormal experience before in his life, thinking he might just be one of those sorts of people who have strange things happening to them all the time. He said strangely enough he hadn't until last Wednesday 25th February, the day before the invoice was discovered. He was working in Halifax surveying an office and had to do some inspections upstairs. The ladies on the counter could not leave the shop unattended as they were short staffed, so they asked him if he could go upstairs on his own. He entered one of the rooms where they keep all the brochures and in the corner stood a lady with her back to him. She had long black curly hair and wore a long black skirt. He thought it was a real person so apologised for intruding to which she didn't reply.

On returning back downstairs he asked the ladies on the counter about the women upstairs, they just looked at each other and simply replied "you must have seen Janet", the nickname they had given this familiar apparition. This was the first time in his life he had ever experienced anything like this.

Finally after an hour or so we all agreed the whole thing was totally unexplainable so decided to just see if anymore strange events would happen. As he left we agreed to contact each other with any new information that may arise.

On Sunday 7th March my sister was going through her university notes when she noticed a printed sheet in her design and planning folder with a list of people's names. In one of the groups at the bottom of the list was the name of Adam's ex-girlfriend. She asked around at university the next day but no one has seen her since before Christmas, in fact she should have been there that day. My sister has never met her, as she is not in her group. I asked if Adam would contact her but as far as I know he hasn't just yet.

I don't know if any of this has anything to do with my sister's house as a few strange things seem to be happening there. Charlie hears footsteps running round in the bedroom next to hers which is empty at the moment. I too have had the same experience in that room about eleven years ago as did my younger sister.

Just this week Charlie was touched on the arm by an invisible force and had an instant image in her mind, like a memory. It was of a woman with blonde hair tied back in a bun standing on some steps leading up to a house holding a baby.

THE GRINNING GHOST

Here is my true ghost story and I am still suffering the effects of it to this day, playing the same event over in my mind. Before witnessing the ghost, I would have to say that I was a big sceptic but on seeing it I have changed my mind. The sighting occurred on the 20th October 1999 at 10:30pm on the B2036. A road that runs from Haywards Heath to Crawley, eventually joining the A23 to Crawley. My personal view is that you do not find ghosts, they find you.

My best mate and I were driving back from his house, I had not been drinking, nor had I taken any substances that could have caused it. The moon was coming out from behind a cloud and there was heavy rain on the road surfaces. We had been driving for something like thirty to forty minutes and had joined the B2036, which goes through ancient woodland, and becomes nothing more than a country lane at that point.

The woodland itself is called Worth Forest.

I looked at my watch and the time said 10:30pm and I can remember that I was relaxed and not thinking of anything in particular. The car in front had disappeared and its headlights had faded into the darkness, so we were effectively the only vehicle on that unlit stretch of the road. It was then that I noticed in the car headlight beams, some distance ahead an owl flying across the road, that had come from the hedgerow, as if startled by something. On closer examination as we approached, I saw a misty patch, like fog emanating slowly from the grass verge on the right.

I did not think anything about it too much, except that the next events took me by surprise.

In no less than four seconds this misty patch, took on a life of its own, I would have to say a supernatural presence. The misty patch expanded in size so rapidly that it became a dense threatening thick wall of fog that spread right across the right hand side of the road. This I now know was no ordinary fog, but was like 'ectoplasm'.

As the fog cleared and disappeared I could see something moving ahead in front of the car headlights. I could clearly see it was a cowled figure like a monk that appeared to be intent on crossing the road from the right hand side. It had not seen us approaching at this stage, and had it arms outstretched. To my horror after examining the situation I saw that the figure was not walking like a normal human but 'gliding' just above the road surface. I was also having trouble clearly delineating it, because as it got to the centre line it disappeared and reappeared again in exactly the same spot and repeated the same action, time and time again. The ghost I would have to say took on a clearly ethereal appearance.

As we drew closer in the car I started to worry as to whether my friend had seen it, so I had decided to observe it and say nothing, because I feared he would crash the car. Watching again, I saw that it had observed us and was now aware of us. Our headlights were illuminating it as we drew closer to it. Now the ghost reached the centre reservation line, stopped and turned to face us head on.

I could see that it was now transparent to semi invisible. The headlight beams of our vehicle shone through it and I could see the rain falling on the other side, and the road disappearing off into the distance.

As we drew closer still the ghost decided to move, and now glided across to the left hand side of the road i.e. passenger side where I was seated. Some distance ahead the ghost now 'decided' to reveal itself. To my horror a full ghost dematerialised in front of the vehicle on my side. All I can say is that I have never experienced pure terror like that, my heart was thudding and I wanted to say something to my friend who was driving, but found that I could not get any words out. So I kept quiet, as all the time we drew nearer to it.

The ghost was of a portly middle aged man, I would say in his forties to fifties. I got the impression that he did not belong to this century, as his clothes were dated. Around his waist there was a belt with a buckle and he wore large boots. I got the impression that he may have been a highway robber because the man was bald, and he had an earring in his right ear. He was standing there just grinning widely, I could see in his lower jar there were gold fillings. He wore a stripy 'jumper' like the 'Bretons' wear in Brittany France, and a necktie.

I sat there dumbfounded and I could not believe what I was seeing. I thought I must be hallucinating so when I shut my eyes and reopen them it will have gone. I shut my eyes took some deep breaths reopened them, and the figure was still there grinning in the middle of the road! By now I was beginning to panic a though crossed my mind what if we hit it.

As we approached rapidly I started to fear that we were going to collide with it. I heard stories that ghosts sometimes go right through vehicles. I therefore started to will in my mind for it to disappear, but it would not go. I realised that if it did not go we would hit it. As we reached the point of no return a few metres from it, the ghost just vanished, dematerialising as suddenly as it had come.

We were now level with the spot where the ghost had been standing. I checked the side windows of the car, as we passed to see if someone had been playing a trick. I also looked back out of the window in the back. All I could see was an eerie, empty lonely road, with the autumn leaves falling slowly down into the road. We were now completely alone.

ANOTHER ROAD GHOST

November 1985, imagine if you can a cool crisp November evening the sort of evening that the moon is close and sits low in the sky, you can see your breath but it's not quite freezing.

It was a night like this that I experienced one of the most vivid and terrifying experiences that I have ever had. I had been dating a girl in one of the neighbouring villages for some weeks.

I lived in the village of Slyne-with-Hest at the time and she lived about six miles away in Nether Kellet Nr Carnforth. The journey there would take some time, as all I had for transport was a rather old Puch 50 Moped - the really naff one with the pedals!

Anyway the normal route that I would take would be through the village of Bolton-Le-Sands to a pub called The Blue Anchor, then turn right and make my way from their to Nether Kellet.

It wasn't the journey there that was the problem, it was when I decided to come home.

As I said earlier about the conditions, it was a full moon lighting up the road which ran through farmland.

As I approached a long right hand bend, the lights on the moped dimmed to a sidelight, so unsuspecting anything untoward I tapped the headlight thinking that it could be a loose connection. The light stayed as it was so I continued on with my journey. I rounded a corner and passed a rise in the road which had an old tree on the left and as I got to the brow of the hill, she appeared before me. A Victorian women in a hooped dress with a bodice top which had lacing up the back. I could see the ghost in great detail, her hair was put up and there were ringlets coming down from a bun at the back.

I was travelling at a slow twenty miles per hour so I was gaining on her.

I seem to remember that their was no colour to the figure, just grey with lots of detail. You could tell that the dress was hooped because of how it came out from the bodice there was a bow at the back.

I was scared to death my eyes transfixed on the figure that was getting closer and closer I never saw her face. I must have got about five to ten feet from her and she turned and went through the hedge. As I passed the spot I became more afraid that she might come after me. I travelled a few metres and then to scare me even more the lights that were dim on the moped then came back on. This frightened me again after what I had just seen. I was so scared that I nearly crashed the bike on the sharp hairpin corner coming down the hill.

I forgot to put the pedal down on the opposite side to the corner that I was taking!!

I got to the junction at the bottom of the road and took of my helmet and smoked a cigarette to try and calm me down. I felt reassured, as there were streetlights now as there were none before. The only problem that I then had was that I had to drive the moped past two graveyards!

I wasn't drunk and had not taken any drugs before you doubt the story. I didn't go out looking for ghosts it was pure coincidence it just happened.

THE SEA CAPTAIN'S HOUSE

We bought a house near Hull which was built early 1900's, these houses were built for Sea Captains and Pilots amongst other professional people.

We renovated the house and made the loft holes bigger to enable us to store things in the loft. There were two lofts and the one at the back was quite small, not big enough to stand up in. When we looked in there we found an old fashioned candle holder with a candle and spent matches still in it and alongside an old bible. In this bible various phrases were underlined so we fetched these out of the loft, and kept them downstairs.

This is when things started to happen. I was not nervous about being in the house on my own, but I didn't like going upstairs, and I would always use the downstairs toilet when I was on my own. My dog used to sit and growl sometimes, and when we had glass doors put in internally she used to sit and look into the hallway through the glass doors, and growl with all her hair standing up on end.

Then one night I had gone to bed early with a migraine, and my husband came in from the pub, and woke me up, he told me that I wasn't asleep as the light was on in the middle bedroom. I replied "I was asleep and he must have been imaging it!"

One time my son and girlfriend stayed one night and woke up with a feeling the house was on fire, the room was full of smoke, but when they put the light on there was nothing there.

One night we had been out for a meal, and we came back with friends. Later they went home and we went to bed. Early hours of the morning I awoke and wanted to go to the bathroom, I am not scared of the dark, so I didn't turn any lights on. I walked down the landing into the bathroom put the light on, when I had finished I was just about to turn the bathroom light off, and walk back, when a man walked along the landing passed me, and went into the back bedroom.

I walked back (thinking it was my son and that he came home late) got into bed, and laid a bit then it suddenly hit me, my son was not coming back he was staying at his girlfriend's house! So I awoke my husband and explained what had happened, and we had a laugh saying it must have been Marley.

I was not scared, and I used to say I don't know who you are but you don't scare me but we had a lot of bad luck, my husband lost his job, then I lost mine. I had two miscarriages, my father died, the dog died, we had two bikes stolen. In the end I sensed that this was an unhappy house and that we would do no good until we moved.

So we put the house up for sale, and moved out about one year later. When I moved out I was unpacking and noticed the candle holder, and the bible had been taken with us to our new house, and I had a feeling about these items carrying bad luck, so I threw them away, and I sensed the entity had gone away forever.

Afterwards my Mother came to visit us in our new home and stayed the night. I related to her what I had seen, and she asked me if I had noticed she had only stayed one night with us in that house? I did remember and we had put her in the back bedroom with her dog, but she had said there had been a presence in there with her all night, and she had not slept a wink vowing never to stay again. She didn't like telling us because we had to live there and live with whatever was haunting the Sea Captain's House.

MY TWO EXPERIENCES

I have had a couple of strange experiences in my house that I would like to share.

The first one I remember clearly was about six years ago, my family has always kept dogs and unfortunately one of them became ill and died. The whole family was very upset especially as the dog had died overnight at the vets and we didn't get a chance to say goodbye. That night me and my mum were the last people to go to bed, I had just pulled the covers over me and switched the light off when I felt a dog jump off the bed (this was strange as our dogs always slept in my parents room, and none of the dogs had been in my room). I looked up to see my little dog who had died that day. I sat upright in bed and watched as she walked across my bedroom, out of the door and over the landing. She distinctly looked back towards me then walked through my parents open bedroom door just as my mum was closing it. When I told my mum she said she hadn't seen a thing. I like to think it was her way of saying goodbye.

The second incident had two other witnesses. My parents were away on holiday and I had two friends staying over. We were in the living room listening to CDs when me and one of my friends heard a loud whistle that sounded like it was near the door at the other end of the room. We both looked at each other and told our other friend to turn the volume down on the CD player, she turned it off and we sat in silence for a few seconds but heard nothing else. We thought it might be something outside so I was just about to pull the curtain open to look when all three of us heard a huge, loud bang in the room directly above us (this happens to be my parents bedroom), like someone had dropped a very large heavy object. All of us jumped up and ran out of the house as fast as we could. Once outside we all stood staring at the house, I telephoned my grandparents and they were round very quickly. They checked the house top to bottom and found nobody else there and nothing was out of place in my parent's room.

About a year later when I was alone in the house cooking dinner, I heard the same whistle directly behind me but could not see anything. I was terrified and ran to the front door but remembered it was locked and my keys were in my handbag upstairs. I started shaking and grabbed the telephone to call someone but suddenly I felt angry and annoyed so I said out loud: "This is my house and I'm not going to let anything scare me in my own home." I then walked back into the kitchen and carried on cooking as normal but spent the rest of the night feeling very uneasy.

There have been two other times when I thought I have heard a very faint whistling sound but now I do not feel scared when I hear it. My friends still refuse to stay at my home two years later.

THE CANAL BUILDING GHOST

While at lunch today we began remembering when we used to work in an old Sheffield building next to the canal called 'The Straddle'. The reason it's called this is that it straddles the canal. Built in the 1800s it was originally a warehouse - the canal boats would go under the building and their cargoes would be winched off (the old winching gear still exists.) The building has been sympathetically redeveloped so you can still see the holes in the floor where the barges would wait under (now glass parts of the floor.)

Whilst we were occupying this building a strange thing happened to one of the receptionists, she told me about it the next day.

The reception area is on the first floor in a very well lit area. Two receptionists were on duty at the time - it was around lunchtime. The receptionist who saw the 'ghost' was stood by the reception desk, the other was sitting down at the desk. The former told me how she had been stood there when she sensed that someone had come up to her out of the corner of her eye. She assumed that it was a member of staff wanting her for something, but when she turned to see who it was, she saw a man. She could describe him quite clearly - dark with a Roman nose, and wearing something which looks like hessian. She was surprised by the man and quickly looked to the other receptionist to alert her. When she looked back (and this was in a matter of a moment) he had disappeared. She said that nothing like that had ever happened to her before.

I would say that the lady in question was a credible witness - a highly respected employee. The building had very tight security and electronic passes were required to enter not only the building, but also to each floor of it. Also, a security guard would have been present at the main entrance so I wouldn't expect someone to have wandered in - even if he had, how did he disappear?

The thing that stood out for me was that she said he was wearing hessian. I remember seeing something in a museum about bargeworkers in the 19th century, that they tended to cover themselves with hessian as the job was so filthy. I don't know if the receptionist knew that.

NORTH YORKSHIRE GHOST

I know a great deal about one of the most haunted halls in North Yorkshire. Sadly to protect its identity I have had to change its name and of its owners. This story was collected from a close family member who details as a series of incidents.

Once an old abbey, the house has many interesting stories attached to it, that I have been unfortunate enough to encounter first hand.

On one of the many occasions that I stayed at the house, I learnt the numerous curses and legends and experienced the sometimes very hostile paranormal activity there.

The children's (now adults) playroom was a room called The Sun Room. This was named as such due to a trapeze shaped box padlocked onto the middle of the mantle piece which you will still find there. Under this box, there is reputedly a bible. Anyone who removes this bible will gradually get sicker until, if the bible is not replaced, they will die. The last time this was allowed to happen was about a hundred years ago, when a guest to the house fell very ill. A maid attending to something in her room noticed on her bedside table the bible. She immediately replaced it and the women recovered from near death within a day.

Having spent a large amount of time in this room I can vouch for certain incidents that have happened whilst I have been there.
Though the room is always cold, I do not necessarily attribute this to paranormal activity - the house is after all around four hundred years old.

On two occasions I have felt something grab me in this room. The first occasion, I was alone. It was about 7:00pm on a dark winters night and I was eating pizza and drinking a beer. Julia (the daughter of the family) had left the room for some reason. As I fast-forwarded through the trailers at the beginning of a film, I felt a freezing cold hand grab my wrist. It was hard and I dropped the remote with the pain. Sarah walked into the room and immediately commented on the temperature of the room. When I told her what had happened, we also noted that my right hand was still freezing cold towards the wrist and on the wrist. The other hand was fine.

The other occasion, when I personally felt something there was a lot of us in the room. There had been a party and around six or seven of us were sleeping off the night's festivities in the The Sun Room. I had managed to get the sofa, a friend of mine Patrick was on the armchair next to me, someone else in the other armchair and a few people on the floor. Though I usually feel uncomfortable left alone in that room - or even with people if it is dark, I was not feeling remotely bothered that night (most likely due to a lot of beer.) I felt perfectly calm and fell asleep to the amusing grunts and snores of the men folk in the room. It was about three hours later, around four in the morning, when I awoke - irritated to what appeared to be Patrick's hand sneaking its way up my thigh. I was again freezing cold. I opened my eyes and tried to work out how Patrick was reaching me. I couldn't make sense of the situation at all, so I sat up to tell him to get off. At this point I realised that he was still fast asleep, and no-one was in a position to reach my leg. The worst thing was there still appeared to be an area of pressure on my thigh. At this point I panicked and slapped my thigh hard a few times. The pressure miraculously lifted - just like someone taking their hand off my leg. I must have yelped out loud because another male friend woke up and asked me what the matter was. He decided to come over and share a cigarette while we talked about it and it was when he took a cigarette off me to light, he noticed how freezing cold I was. I had been fine when I went to sleep, and indeed, the room seemed a reasonable temperature.

The Sun Room is not the only centre for paranormal activity in the house. The old corridor is at the part of the house the family live in (other parts are shown to the public) and is long and narrow, with about three guest bedrooms all with ensuite bathrooms along it. It is in the old part of the house and the bedrooms look out over the gardens and park at the back. I have never experienced any discomfort walking down this corridor, or in these bedrooms, and the temperature always feels normal but the corridor has become less of a scary situation but more of a nuisance for the family. For about ten years, with increasing noise, persistence and ferocity, children's laughing and sometimes crying has been heard in the corridor accompanied by the sounds of people running around. Frequently, the same phenomenon occurs - the sound of a crying, angry child, running down the full length of the corridor away from the drawing room, where they watch TV in the evenings, towards the kitchen before finally, the kitchen door slams with astonishing violence. The family are totally used to this, and generally roll there eyebrows in a 'oh its having a tantrum again' manner. However, quite frequently, Julia's mother has appeared in the Sun Room (far away at the other end of the corridor) to enquire as to whether we are alright and whether it was the ghost or us interrupting their evening.

The kitchen in the house is not the original, they do use the original kitchen but only for catering for big parties and shoots etc. The day-to-day kitchen is in the apartments the family use. It is small and cosy with a big aga, and permanent fixtures - a dog and a cat, in front of it. It is not remotely eerie. One day, about three years ago, Julia and her mother left me sitting in the kitchen reading a magazine as they left to go down to the laundry which is located far away from the kitchen. As I sat at the table reading, I became aware of the dog and the cat, who were both, not scared, but had been disturbed by something. Neither was panicked but both had the air of irritancy of an animal told to move. They both slunk away from the aga towards where I was sitting. It was at this point that the large metal spoon, that had been in a huge catering sized vat of chilli con carne or something, flipped out of the vat landed on the floor and proceeded to skid at speed to my feet, where, it promptly stopped millimetres away from the end of my foot. The animals trotted out of the room annoyed with the noise and I remained exactly where I was in total shock, trying to work out how this could have happened. I eventually got up and put the spoon back, trying to work out if there was any rational explanation of how a spoon, who's end is so much heavier than the top, and that had only about two inches out of twelve sticking out of the pan, could have flipped like that. I was still standing over the pan puzzling, when Julia and her Mother walked back into the room and enquired as to why the cat and the dog, were sulking by a radiator in the hall as opposed to their usual beanbags by the aga. I explained what had happened, at which point, totally unperturbed, Julia said "Oh its one of them again is it - next time it happens just throw the spoon back - that's what I do."

Another spectre frequently seen, but seemingly only by women and girls so far, is a little girl around ten or eleven years old sitting on a swing near the ornamental lake at the front of the house. Whether a swing ever hung in this tree is not certain, but it is certainly suitable. She is only ever seen at dusk, smiling, but some have described her as 'troubled'. From the description of her clothes, I would place her between 1780 and 1850.

The weirdest story of the house has created major architectural problems. The last time I was at the house visitors were allowed to walk through this room, though whether it is still safe to do so, I am not sure. This room is called the 'Unfinished Room', and for a good reason.

The story goes, that in the fire, which consumed a couple of rooms on the first floor a few hundred years ago, a maid cursed the room and the family. She had, as was so often the case, been having an affair with the eldest son of the family. As the fire began to roar around them (I am not sure how it started) the eldest son began to save the guests and family members. Despite having been telling the maid that he was desperately in love with her for months, he left her to burn, as he jumped out a window to save himself. As she was watched by the crowd outside, in the paneless window, she cursed the son and the family, declaring that if anyone ever tried to restore the room, to its former glory, the eldest son of the family would die.

This has now happened on two occasions – the first about one hundred years ago, when the eldest son died in a hunting accident the day the work started. You can still see where they stopped work abruptly. The family have never attempted again, and the room still stands with burnt walls and part of the floor boards missing.

The final, and most disturbing story of the house (though I was not there to witness this) rests with Julia, daughter of the house, who at the time was a teenage girl.

She was in her then bedroom at the far end of the house, sitting on her bed reading the back of a CD box. Her cat was on the bed next to her. As she read, the door burst open violently and the cat leapt off the bed and onto the back of the sofa against the wall. The cat was clearly very disturbed, with stereotypical arched back and hair on end. What was more eerie was that the cat was clearly watching something or someone - something Julia could not see. As the cat's eyes followed this invisible force to the dressing room all hell broke loose. Deodorant cans and hairbrushes began lifting up above the dressing table before slamming back down on their sides, knocking everything else off.

She watched in horror as the cat began to growl and 'watch' the thing move towards the bed where she was sitting. At this point she began to yell for her mother as she watched the bedclothes being 'pulled at' off the bed. Her Mother hearing the screams arrived pretty quickly and watched in horror as something started to pull at the clothes on Sarah, and the cat yowled and watched. This went on for a few more moments when eventually, her mother felt something brush past her, the ashtray on Julia's bed fell to the floor and everything stopped. The cat ran under the bed and Julia, now in a hysterical state fell back onto the bed from where she had been trying to escape.

Now I did not witness this and I admit that it is a story a teenage girl could make up. It is not something I believe however, that a fourty eight year old well respected member and Lady of the community would back up such a colourful story. Especially if she was describing the distressful situation her daughter was in.

Above are just the choice picks from a house plagued with slamming doors, mysterious people brushing past, a house where at least once a day you find yourself talking to someone in the corner of your eye, who turns out not to be there. An old and mysterious house, with some very, very unpleasant atmospheres, whilst at other times, simply playful.

NORMAN RETURNS

I feel compelled now to tell you of my experience of working in a nursing home when I was eighteen. I am now twenty five and still cannot look at the nursing home whilst driving past.

I used to work the weekend night shifts with one other care assistant and a nurse. Even when I worked the day shifts the feeling of somebody behind me was intolerable. It didn't matter if it were day or night.

There were many experiences and feelings I felt, but there is one that stands out from all the rest.

It all happened when on a very hot July day, an old man called Norman died in his room. He had Alzheimers, so his death was a sweet relief for him I'm sure.

Anyway, Norman had a particular smell in life. His wife used to tell us that he had been a very smart man and always dressed in a shirt and tie no matter what the weather. So, at her request, that was how he was dressed by the staff of the home. Because of this he often had a very hot, sweaty smell. Not the ordinary sweaty smell, but somewhat cheesy. His room would smell terrible after a day of Norman sitting in there.

He was the first person I ever saw dead and I didn't come across him in a very nice way after his death. On a very warm day the emergency call bell was ringing from his room. Naturally, I rushed there as quick as I could as the emergency bell obviously means that someone needs help immediately. On entering the room, Yinka, our lovely Nigerian nurse was holding Norman's head up from the pillow on the bed he was laying on. His eyes and mouth were open. Yinka didn't expect it to be me, as I hadn't worked there for long and was relatively inexperienced. He apologised to me and I couldn't understand why at first. Then Yinka told me that Norman had died a few minutes previous. I must admit it was a hell of a shock. I think it was because his eyes and mouth were open. I left the room and went back to see him after he had been washed and prepared by more experienced staff.

After the events I took a few days off work. On my return, I entered the room Norman had died in and was overwhelmed by the smell of Norman. I left immediately and gently complained that the room was smelly still, and maybe it should be spring-cleaned. The matron informed me that this had already been done. The carpets...everything in the room had been stripped and cleaned thoroughly to remove Norman's poignant smell.

I was disturbed by this, but not really frightened.

As the weeks went on, the smell got worse. I got worse too, I would no longer go upstairs to collect residents belongings alone. I was frightened to walk to the laundry room at the back of the house on my own. Everybody thought I was going mad, but I knew inside I wasn't. I had an intolerable fear...like there was always someone behind me, I was forever looking over my left shoulder.

Norman's room was one of three in a short little corridor on the ground floor of the house. As time went on, the smell of his room, which I incidentally would no longer enter, moved from the room to the corridor. It became so bad that all you had to do was open the glass door to the corridor and you would be overwhelmed by a hot sweaty smell.

At this time, other people started to see exactly what I had been talking about. The room was cleaned constantly...but to no avail. It was eventually deemed unfit to show this room to prospective residents and was used as the 'death' room. The room was used for people who needed a lot of tending to prior to death, and as it was very accessible being on the ground floor, it was used solely for that purpose.

After all this, and just before I left the home at Christmas, other things started to happen. Bells would ring in rooms that were unoccupied. Voices were heard from the top of corridors. That was enough for me, I left without looking back. I was terrified.

Interesting enough, about two years after working at the home, I started working in another one about fifteen miles away.

One evening, I went into a room with two other members of staff to tend to a lady called Iris. There wasn't anything mentally wrong with this lady. She had a brain operation that left her debilitated physically...but certainly not mentally.

On entering the room, Iris shouted at me to get out. As I had never met her before, I thought this was quite strange. The other staff asked her why she did not want me in her room. She said as clear as day, "Because she's got a strange man following her and I don't like it". Needless to say, two days later I told the matron I did not think I would be happy there.

I now have changed my career path altogether and work in the customer centre of a big mobile phone company. Still helping people which is what I love to do...but in a different way!

HEADLESS DOG OF MANCHESTER

Just thought I would contact you with something inexplicable which happened recently and which left myself and my partner feeling a little unnerved to say the least!

We decided to go to the cinema, and were driving through Manchester to get to the Odeon Cinema in Peter/Oxford Street. We were driving along Gloucester Street, which is quite deserted at night and as we were driving, (my partner was the driver) something caught my eye. There is a building in Gloucester Street by the canal near a railway bridge and that is where I noticed something moving.

Before I really focus on the object, I was aware it was heading towards us, as I focused and realised what the object was, it had turned so I observed it forty five degrees on. It was a dog, turning into what I thought was an archway. I commented to my partner that it was a large dog which he then noticed. It disappeared into the 'archway' and we both observed it's front flank and the rest of the body apart from the head. Our car was within a second of the archway which suddenly revealed itself as a door painted in deep blue.

We suddenly realised that we had witnessed the animal passing through a solid object. Both of us drove for a few seconds before saying anything, but we both realised something strange had happened. Hairs on the back of the neck and all that. We visited the building after the cinema and made sure that it was a door which indeed it was. The actual building was Hotspur house in Gloucester Street, the time we saw the dog was at 7:35pm on Thursday the 24th August.

One thing that struck us, was that we did not see the head of the dog and looking on the internet have revealed that there was a headless dog in the nineteenth century, which regularly appeared in Manchester. It has become albeit briefly, a flurry of discussion amongst us and our friends and family, but I have to admit that it has affected us more than we care to let on.

THE HAUNTED HOLIDAY

It was in September 1995 that my wife and I went for a week's self-catering holiday to Weymouth. Other family members should have accompanied us but they had to cancel at short notice. The accommodation was a flat above a shop on the sea front. We were greeted on arrival by the owner who said he hoped we would not feel too lonely as the accommodation consisted of three floors.

One gained entry from the street via a door and down a stone flagged passage, then through another door and up a flight of stairs into the living room. This room was very nicely furnished and thick carpeted, as were the kitchen on the next floor up and the two bedrooms above that. The bathroom was also on the top floor. Though I am not normally a fanciful or nervy person but I must admit to a slight uneasy feeling as soon as we entered the first flight of stairs, though it was a bright sunny day, but we were very pleased when we saw what a pleasant living room it was. There was a big bay window overlooking the promenade and you could not wish for a better view.

After unpacking I went up to the bathroom on the top floor to have a wash and shave and while shaving I had an overpowering sensation that someone was behind me, so much so that the hair on the back of my head stood on end. This bathroom was a long narrow room, about six foot wide and twenty feet long, the sink and toilet were at the far end of the room. I remember thinking if the light bulb blew at night it would be awkward to get to the door, as there were no windows except a tiny sky light.

This feeling of being watched occurred every time I went into the bathroom. On returning to the living room my wife asked what the hell had I been doing to make such a racket upstairs? She said it sounded like I was dragging the drawers about on the wooden floorboards, to which I replied that it must have been next door.

I did not mention the feeling that I had in the bathroom so as not to make her uneasy. We later found out that the property next door was a lock up shop that closed at six o'clock so would have been empty at the time my wife heard the noise. To add to my feeling of unease my wife told me that when she was using the bathroom, she could hear what sounded like two or three people whispering. I told her it was most likely the wind blowing in through the skylight.

The next unnerving thing was when I was looking out of the bay window admiring the view. I suddenly had the distinct feeling that something was behind me and going to push me through the window. I thought this place is beginning to get to me and I had better pull myself together.

The noises continued every night and from the second night onwards we slept with the light on all night. I made the excuse that it would be easier to get to the bathroom. That was the first time I have slept with a light on since I was a child. There was lots of other odd things that occurred but two stand out the most in my memory. I thought I saw a man in top hat and tails standing at the living room door, though at the time I thought it was my imagination but the strangest thing happened on the fourth night of our stay.

We had been out for a drink but only had two halves of lager so we would not have to go to the bathroom in the middle of the night. We had just sat down with a cup of tea and were watching the television when all of a sudden there was one hell of an explosion, so powerful that the building shook and we almost spilled our drinks.

The first thing I thought was that the gasometer which was about half a mile away had exploded and I ran to the window expecting to see the sky lit up by fire. To my amazement all seemed normal and quiet.

The following morning we were in the market and got talking to two young girls who were working on one of the stalls and I asked if they had heard the terrific explosion the night before and though they lived nearby they had heard nothing.

Well after that we hated going back to the flat at night and though we were booked until Saturday we left for home at four in the morning on the Friday. As we pulled away I remarked to the wife that I had never been so glad to get away from a place before.

When I told her of the things I had experienced she said it was a good thing I did not say anything before or she would have left right away, as she had also felt very frightened but had not said anything thinking I would ridicule her.

I am an ex-soldier with many years service and I am used to the sound of heavy gunfire but the explosion we heard at Weymouth was more like a very powerful bomb.

THE HAUNTED MARSHES

A very strange vision 'seemed' to appear while I was walking the dog on part of what is left of the Rainham Marshes in Essex.

I live on the 'Mardyke Estate' in Rainham and could have sworn I saw a large fat figure with no head while I walked the dog around the fields adjacent to our block of flats! The figure appeared to be about seventy-five metres away from me and was directly in front of me as I walked along the 'flood barrier path' which circles an expanse of grass behind a block of maisonettes on the estate.

I kept walking, as the dog was well ahead of me, perhaps ten metres from the figure. However, when I got within about fifteen metres from the figure (the dog having run straight past it) it seemed to almost evaporate. When I actually walked through the area where I'd seen it, I smelt a very strong odour of what I can only compare to joss sticks or some form of incense.

The dog had not reacted in any way unusual as he passed the figure, but on the way back, he became very agitated and aggressive as we passed the area where I believed I'd seen the figure. This is very unlike my dog, who is very old and placid.

The smell was no longer obvious as I passed the spot but I felt incredibly cold and ill at ease. I fully admit that this may well have been due to my own apprehension at passing through the area again, but shortly before I actually exited the field, I am sure I heard a really haunting laughing.

The dog again became unusually aggressive and vocal and it took me a while to calm him enough to get him to come to me and put a lead on him. My girlfriend seems totally 'unimpressed' by my story and says I more than likely 'imagined' the whole sequence of events.

WEIRD EXPERIENCES

Ever since an early age I have had happenings and sightings of ghosts. When I was three I was upstairs and a gorilla's hand came from under the chair, then when I ran downstairs something popped out of the ground that looked like a transparent, colourful devil.

When I was around seven I was often woken up to something jumping underneath my bed and once saw something invisible banging my Barbie doll against my record player.

My mum took me to the doctors because she was worried about me but of course the doctor said it was my imagination.

I have seen black figures brush against the clothes horse and the clothes move with it so I know it's not my eyes playing tricks on me. I have had the feeling of being held down in bed whilst something like the sound of keys rattled in my ears and also the feeling of wanting to get out of bed but at the same time pulled back.

Every house we have lived in has had the smell of fish coming from the landing and we read that poltergeists leave strange smells. Only last night I was woken up to my dresser next to my bed being shook and I know I wasn't dreaming because my bangle on my dresser was still rattling when I sat up in bed.

HAUNTED AIRFIELDS

My wife Pauline and I have had several rather strange experiences with airfields in the last couple of years. It is fair to say that we are both quite sensitive to the paranormal, and have both seen ghosts in the past.

Firstly, RAF Spilsby which is about eight miles west of Skegness. It used to be a wartime bomber base, long disused and the runway now cut by two narrow roads. Pauline and I decided to go and take some photographs of the runway and the buildings while we were in the area a couple of years ago.

We got out of the car and within seconds experienced the usual symptoms, and we just knew that something was going to happen. We then heard a low-pitched rumbling - the unmistakeable sound of a Lancaster bomber. Our first reaction was "Battle of Britain Flight". However, the noise got louder and louder, and despite the cloud cover being very thin, we could see no aeroplane even though two minutes passed. Then, just as it seemed unthinkable that the noise could be so loud without an aircraft being visible, the noise instantly changed to that of a jet, and a Tornado whizzed over at low level, presumably en route to the coastal bombing ranges. A very disturbing experience. We were not, and indeed are still not, aware of any other paranormal reports related to RAF Spilsby.

Another strange experience happened at East Kirkby. The runway ghost with the trailing parachute is well documented. We have never seen him, but are convinced that this unfortunate man is not the only presence on the airfield, for reasons that I will explain.

On our first holiday visit to East Kirkby, we had all the usual symptoms while walking around the display hangar and even worse in the control tower, so much so, that Pauline could not bear to stay in it any longer. It was as if somebody was following a couple of paces behind.

After our holiday we returned to our home in Stockport, and thought nothing more of it. That was until one evening, we saw a television documentary about East Kirkby and "Just Jane" the Lancaster. The museum is of course owned by the Panton brothers. The documentary went on to talk about Christopher, the Panton brother who was killed during the Nuremberg raid. The room temperature dropped, the hairs stood on end. A photograph of Christopher came up on the screen. I knew immediately and turned round to look at Pauline and said "he's the presence at the airfield". She said "yes, and he's in this room at this very moment". We saw nothing, but the feeling changed slightly, almost as an acknowledgement of our recognition.

Since then, we have had several experiences of Christopher Panton visiting us. The most recent was in August this year when we were driving along in our people carrier talking about air museums. The feeling was so strong that our teenage daughter was convinced that someone was sitting in the back of the vehicle with her.
In conclusion, I am sure that Christopher means us no ill. I just wish that I could do something to help him rest in peace. Perhaps I could, but can't yet see what it is.

MORE AIRFIELD GHOSTS

Prior to moving to Lincolnshire in the mid-1990's I lived in the county along with my wife (at the time in question) and visited East Kirkby. My wife experienced similar feelings especially upstairs. I too have encountered and sensed similar feelings myself on the first floor landing especially the first room on the right-hand side.

The only other airfield control tower building I have no wish to visit again is the former Colby Grange control tower on the A15 between Lincoln and Sleaford.

Prior to entering the control tower I sensed as if I was being watched and the feeling was even greater on the first floor at the front. Standing in the middle of this room I very much felt as if I was unwelcome. Turning my head sharply in the direction of where I felt someone was standing just for a split second I saw a dark figure/shadow.

I again felt the same feeling as inside when I walked from left to right round the front of the control tower. It felt as if someone was watching me from the balcony again, on sharply turning my head looking up just for a second I saw the same figure.

Over the years I have visited many former wartime airfields and have never before encountered a feeling of being unwelcome or for a second seeing anything. Yes, I have sensed I have not been alone on one or two occasions but nothing else other than that.

BLACK MAGICK GHOST

This happened back in 1997, my now ex-wife and I had just moved into our new house in a village in the middle of Milton Keynes, the village is quite old with some parts of it dating back to the thirteenth century.

However the house we were moving into was built in 1984.

We moved, it was a nice house and the first months we lived there we had no problems. One day we had a issue with the water tank in the loft, as I was climbing up through the hatch I happened to spot under the tank a crucifix surrounded by candles. I didn't think anything of it, did what I had to do and climbed back down. I told my wife what I had seen and she was quite distressed by this. She told me I should go back up and remove the offending items. So I did what she asked (for a quiet life!) and she disposed of the candles and crucifix. It turned out afterwards she had broken the cross and thrown it away in the rubbish! I wasn't too happy about it but what had been done, had been done.

This is when the strange things started to happen.

I worked early shifts and was out of the house usually by 4:00am, I got to work around 5:00am and my wife then phoned me at 5:15am. She was very upset and when I managed to calm her down, she told me what had happened after I had left.

She had heard me leave, and was still in bed when she heard the front door to the house open and close, she assumed it was me coming back thinking I had forgotten something and had come back to pick it up. She said she heard footsteps coming up the stairs and into the bedroom, now she was facing with her back to the door so never saw anyone come in to the room, but the covers were lifted and she felt something get into bed with her and cuddle up close, this alarmed her as I wouldn't have come back and got back into bed!

So without turning over she said, "what are you doing back home?" With that whatever was in the bed dissipated and the covers fell flat and she was on her own again, which is when she phoned me.

The second incident happened a few days after that, when I was there, we had gone to bed and both of us had fallen asleep. It must have been a few hours after that, when I was woken up my frantic digs in the ribs by my better half, she whispered to me, "There's someone in the room with us!"

I was a bit sceptical about it all and told her it was her imagination. She was quite certain that there was a person there in the corner of the room squatting down staring at her. That was when she said "Look! He's still there, cant you see him?" I couldn't and told her to go back to sleep. Which we both did and put it down to her imagination.

This happened twice more, I couldn't see anything the first or second time, but the third time frightened my wife and me. Instead of the figure crouching in the corner, it was crouching next to the bed staring right at her. I woke up after sleeping fitfully to see this figure, it was a man and looked like he was wearing a black cloak and no shirt, I couldn't make out any facial features apart from a pair of staring eyes. Whereupon I switched the light on, and it vanished, leaving a strange smell of tobacco smoke and baking bread! I woke up my wife and told her what had just occurred. She was very upset to say the least. That was the last time we saw the crouching man.

Nothing then happened for the next six months or so, until we started to get a small pile of gravel appearing at the foot of the stairs, this was really puzzling as we didn't know where the gravel was coming from! It was perfectly piled into a conical shape about three inches high. It was cleaned up and the next day it was back, this went on for a week, and then stopped as abruptly as it started.

The next and last manifestation that took place was on the top floor, I had been out visiting family and my wife was at home on her own. When I returned, she was (again) in a bit of a state, she was curled up in a ball really distraught. She then told me that after I had left the doors upstairs had started to bang violently. Thinking that she had left the windows open causing a draught, she went upstairs and the doors were all closed but she could still hear the slamming doors! Needless to say that she went back into the sitting room and didn't venture back out. The slamming doors went on for another three quarters of an hour and stopped as suddenly as it had started.

Later that evening, we heard footsteps and doors opening and closing from upstairs. I went up to check and all was quiet, as soon as I went back down into the sitting room it started again. This time it only lasted for ten minutes or so.

Nothing as bad as the things that happened ever occurred again but there was a strange atmosphere in the house, it was oppressive and anyone who came in to visit would say that they felt it also, as if there was a great sadness.

When I split from my wife I moved back with my parents, she sold the house and I always wonder if the present owners have had any strange experiences in the house. I did a bit of investigation into the previous tenants and discovered that there had been a family there, where the grandmother had come to stay and had died in the spare room.

SOUTH WALES HAUNTING

The strangest experience of the supernatural that I have ever experienced was when I was 17 years old. That was in 1970 and at the time I was going out with a very attractive 16-year-old girl, who had a really bubbly, full of fun, personality and in truth I was very fond of her. There was even talk of "engagement" and to all out friends we were "made for each other".

As I wish to keep her identity confidential, I will call her Louise but that is not her real name.

Around 7.00pm Louise called at my house. My parents were out at the time so we decided we'd stay in to watch TV.

At that time I lived in a simple 'two up, two down' terraced house. I'd prefer not to say where it is exactly but it is in South Wales near the seaside and is currently occupied.

After inviting her in, I went to the downstairs kitchen to make us both some coffee. She went in to the middle room and sat down by the fireside. My house had a coal fire in those days and on a cold, crisp autumn evening, sitting in front of a real coal fire was a nice place to be....

The middle room was separated from the kitchen by a sliding door that had "stippled" glass which meant you could see distorted shapes through it but not much else. For some reason, I slid the door behind me when I went into the kitchen and got on with making the coffee. As I glanced up, I saw a dark shape on the other side of the glass, thinking nothing of it, I assumed that it must have been Louise brushing her long, dark hair in the mirror.

Anyway, I made the coffee, slid open the door and entered the middle room with two cups of coffee. To my surprise, Louise was standing by the fireplace facing the chimney breast on which there was a large mirror. I could see from her reflection in the mirror that her face was as white as a sheet. Immediately I knew something was wrong but she wouldn't tell me what it was.

We sat down in the two armchairs that flanked the fireplace and started to drink the coffee. I noticed that she was trembling like a leaf but still she wouldn't tell me why.

Suddenly, without any warning, the room began to get colder and colder until within a matter of just a few minutes you could actually see your our own breath in the icy air. Then I began to smell perfume which was very faint at first but it got stronger and stronger all the time.

After five or ten minutes, the room was very strong with the perfume. It made both of us feel queasy and Louise even started coughing. The cold was getting to be unbearable even though there was a blazing coal fire in the hearth.
These strange events un-nerved me somewhat but they quickly reduced Louise to a quivering wreck. She began to sob hysterically and made it quite clear that she wanted to leave immediately but she still wouldn't (or couldn't) tell me why she was so upset. She just wanted "out".

Even though I had no explanation for the strange events that were taking place, the thought that they could have some strange, supernatural origin never crossed my mind so I simply said to Louise "I tell you what. Let's finish off our coffee in the front room. There's an electric fire in there and we can listen to some music."

Louise agreed to the suggestion without a moment's hesitation.

We went into the front room. I turned on the electric fire and the stereo and we sat together on the settee. We just sat there for about ten minutes holding hands, neither of us saying a word. I guess we were both in shock after the strange events of the previous half hour. The room soon warmed up and gradually Louise regained her composure and, as we began chatting about other things, her face began to lose its deathly pallor.

Suddenly, again without warning, the room began to get colder and colder and Louise began to get increasingly anxious and agitated. Then I could smell the perfume, again, faintly at first, but getting stronger and stronger and this time it was most definitely entering the room from under the door.

I cannot really describe it but you could almost feel it. It was as if there was a huge, solid wave of scent, sickening in it's intensity. That, and the bitter cold, was the straw that broke the camel's back for Louise. She stood up, screamed and ran out of the room, up the short passage and out of the house slamming the front door behind her.

I sat there for a few seconds in absolute shock and disbelief at this latest "twist". For a split second I actually thought that I must be dreaming but the icy atmosphere and the stench of perfume in the front room was all too real.

After what seemed like an eternity, I too stood up and left the room and walked to the front door to go after Louise. As I reached the front door, however, I felt as if someone was standing behind me. My heart began beating like a drum and I stood there frozen to the spot for a few minutes. I wanted to get out of the house but I also felt a strange compulsion to turn around.

Plucking up every ounce of courage in my being, I forced myself to turn round and almost fainted with shock. For there, at the foot of the stairs that faced the front door was the ghost of my paternal grandmother who had died seven years previously and whose house it had been whilst she was alive.

I knew it was Nan immediately because I had lived with her, together with my Mum and Dad in the house from my birth in 1953 until her death in 1963.

Then it really hit me, I was actually looking at a ghost and a ghost was actually looking back at me with a fierce intensity.

I seemed to sense she was angry but curiously I didn't feel that her anger was directed towards me. She remained "solid" and motionless for a good sixty seconds before suddenly disappearing before my very eyes. At that point, my nerve finally broke and I fled the house.

To cut a long story short, I eventually caught up with Louise later that evening at her house and in the comfort of her own surroundings she finally told me what had happened to her earlier in my house.

As I went into the kitchen to make the coffee, she had stood in front of the fire and had begun brushing her hair, suddenly, reflected in the mirror, was what she described as "an old woman dressed in an old fashioned pinky/purple smock with a look of hatred in her eyes".

Then it all began to make sense.

I suddenly realised that the dark shape I had seen through the stippled glass of the kitchen door must have been the ghost of my grandmother and that Louise had seen her ghostly form reflecting back at her in the mirror as she brushed her hair.

No wonder Louise was in such a state when I returned to the room with the coffee. It was a terrible shock to me to think I had seen the ghost of my grandmother who had loved me dearly. God knows what the experience must have been like for Louise who had never known my Nan!

I didn't say a word and pretended that I had no idea of who she could have seen in the mirror particularly as she was so adamant that the old woman she had seen standing behind her clearly wanted her to leave the house and had a "evil look" on her face. .

I couldn't bring myself to tell her what had happened to me after she had fled the house or that she had seen...like me...the ghost of my grandmother. I didn't want to worry her, she'd been through enough.

We stayed together for only a few months more. It was really odd but there was never quite the same "spark" between us after that night and I don't think Louise ever got over it. She refused point blank to enter my house after that night and slowly but surely we drifted apart finally breaking up just before Christmas 1970.

I continued to live in that house until I got married in 1977 and the events of that night were never repeated. My mother and father never experienced anything unusual in the house in all the years they lived there.

The only explanation I can think of is that my grandmother, for some reason, took a dislike to Louise and made her feelings known to her (and to me) that spooky autumn evening in 1970. I have no idea why she disliked her so much but perhaps it was Nan's way of telling me that she wasn't the right girl for me.

CHESHIRE COTTAGE HAUNTING

Forty years ago when my two sons were small we lived in a small cottage in Weston on the outskirts of Crewe Cheshire. A ribbon would appear from the ceiling and float down the stairs, but it was not scary, more the opposite.

My five-year-old son saw it and can still describe it. To me it was pale mauve and see through, however he remembers it as purple. My teenage niece also saw it and said she smelled a lovely flower smell at the same time. I always felt it was a ribbon from a wedding bouquet as it was cut into deep v's at each end.

I had quite forgotten about it, as we had moved away a long time before and my niece and some friends were talking about experiences they had. No one seemed to know of any incident there, but the house had previously been a one up and one down farm cottage and the stairs would have been on the outside.

We thought that as Slaughter Hill is only up the road and many young men were killed there, at the time they would have worn a purple sash.

MJ Wayland writes, "Slaughter Hill is well known for its ghosts and spectres. In local legend it is believed that a Civil War battle took place in a nearby brook which turned red due to all the blood that was spilt. Recently a sword from that period was found, further confirming that something had taken place there."

THE PARANORMAL FOLLOWS ME

I have long since given up trying to explain some of the strange events and sightings that have followed me, the first which happened when I was three years old and the latest was just last night. All of them different and possibly linked to the paranormal. In the very first home I lived in I always had an unexplained fear of the spare bedroom, the door of which opened on to the top of the stairs.

For some reason I decided I wanted to get up in the middle of the night and read a comic downstairs (I was only three) and even though I was so young the memory is so vivid even to this day. As I reached the top of the stairs gripping the rail tightly, I took the first step leaning back slightly so I wouldn't fall and felt a huge shove in my back and went head first roly-poly style all the way down the stairs.

At one point on the stairs I actually remember being upside down holding myself in a teddy style roll in mid air before reaching the bottom in the same position right way up. Without any visible bumps, bruises or marks. Fortunately this was the worst of my experiences, my second home was less eventful apart from the odd door closing by itself and lights switching themselves on.

My first taste of independence in my own flat was more noisy as at certain times of the night I would hear not only the back door opening and closing but also the inner door opening and closing as though some one had come in. Within an hour I would hear them going out and with being a young lass on my own I was too scared to get out of bed and investigate. I was even more scared when I woke to see a shadow of a large person stood in front of the fireplace and then faded away. I never slept in the bedroom again and heard no more sounds or saw any more shadows.

Myself and the lodgers who on occasion shared my last home with me, often heard footsteps upstairs. One poor lad was a complete nervous wreck when left alone for a weekend. On my return he greeted me with "is this house haunted" as he had spent most of the weekend running up and downstairs to see who was up there. When I had a family come to stay with a young girl, her dad was woken during the night by hearing her talking to someone, when he asked who, she replied "the man in the corner" to which he quickly turned the light on but couldn't see any one there.

DON'T STAY

This may sound silly but at my previous address I believe we had ghosts who really didn't want us there.

Firstly, there was always an atmosphere in my house, sometimes my sister and I would be too frightened to look into the corner of our living room and on some occasions we would cry about it, yet we could never explain what was frightening us, and still can't!

Also my Nan's dog before she died kept sniffing in one corner of the room and looking into it as though she was looking at someone. We had cold draughts whiz through a warm room and head towards the corner. We used to hear footsteps up the stairs, the kettle came on and electronic games started up by themselves. I used to feel someone/something sitting on my legs at the bottom of my bed but when I felt around there was nothing there. I dreaded bedtimes as it made me feel physically ill at the thought of enduring another sleepless night fearing what was going to happen.

My mum tried to laugh it off but I could tell she was quite frightened too. One night my sister, brother and I were home alone as my mum had gone out for the evening with friends. We decided to go and watch television in my room instead of staying downstairs as we could hear footsteps and banging coming from upstairs. The quite prominent footsteps marched into my mum's room, the curtains were drawn and it sounded like someone was typing on the computer keyboard. I thought mum must be home, but it's late, why was she on the computer?

Anyway, the noises got louder and other footsteps were coming up the stairs. So we decided to go and check it out. Putting on a brave face I went first and everything in my mum's room was peaceful, yet the noises were still happening and all three of us were terrified. We went back into my room and sat there crying hysterically and then I really lost my temper, I had been living with this fear for ages and I wasn't having it passing on to my siblings so I screamed as loud as I could "for god sake leave us alone we have never done anything to you and you are frightening us. Go away!" And then everything went still, peaceful even. Then for a good few months we were fine, no fear just an oppressive atmosphere but then the noises started again. We have since moved house and I am so very glad as I was so miserable in my old house.

HAUNTED GRAVEYARD

One sunny day in July 1994, my husband and I visited Horsell Woods near Woking, Surrey.

We had heard that there was an World War One Muslim graveyard in Woking and felt that we would like to see it.

However, we took the wrong road to the site, and instead, had to walk through Horsell Woods to reach it. As we walked towards a pond that was situated in the woods, our path was 'crossed' by a figure dressed in backpacking gear. He was taller than I, dressed in dark trousers and a red anorak, and he 'cut across' our path diagonally. He was cut off at the knees, and I didn't see his face, although his hair was dark and he was young, in his 20's.

The surrounding air took on an 'electrical charge' and my hair stood on end. My husband did not see this figure, neither did the dog walkers and the Sunday strollers.

Later, I discovered that this figure had been seen by a friend's mother. I have been back to Horsell Woods since, but have not seen the ghostly figure again.

MJ Wayland writes, "Interestingly Horsell Common has many connections with the paranormal. Firstly its where Martians first land in HG Wells "War of the Worlds" and there are a number of round and long barrows that are alleged to link on a number of ley lines."

HAUNTED PIANO

A friend of mine who lived in Hanwell, London W7 during the 1980's, had a horrible experience involving a piano. He bought a second hand piano, as he was learning to play. The piano duly arrived, accompanied by two old ladies, who, once the piano had been sold, said to one another, 'Will this be an end to it?'

Shortly afterwards, strange goings-on surrounding the piano, began to manifest themselves.

The music holder would shake violently when nobody was near it, and the piano would play one eerie note during the night, when all were in bed. One particularly nasty experience came one night, when the curtains of his bedroom started to flicker and blow as if in a high wind, although no windows were open. The last and final straw came when his sister was attacked by an unseen force, which tried to strangle her.

The piano was given away, and no further experiences reported. My friend believes that the piano was so dear to someone in life, that he/she could not bear to be parted from it. He also told me that while the piano was in the house, the occupants were often sick, and there was an omnipotent malaise that affected the household.

TEXTING GHOST

Our family own an old croft cottage in the Scottish Highlands, which we frequently visit now that it's last occupant (my great-step-grandmother) has died, leaving it to us in her will. Before she lived there, my mother often visited her real grandmother there, over the summer holidays as a child. She was close to her Grandmother, who used to come into her bedroom late every night to check she was OK.

My mother and I visited the cottage together about three years ago, and on the first morning she said she had heard footfalls come up to her bed during the night. She was sure it was Granny, doing what she always did - checking she was OK. She felt nothing but comfort at this, not fear.

Later on, I stayed there with a group of college friends while 'studying' for our exams. One of the girls who was sharing the room where 'Granny' used to sleep, asked the girl she was sharing with why she had been up looking out of the window in the middle of the night. The girl had no idea what she was taking about.

Now, both of these events can be explained rationally. My mother may just have been dreaming or remembering about her Granny coming to visit her as she always did. My college friend may have been sleepwalking. But the weirdest thing that has happened there to date is this.

Last time I was at the cottage, I sent a text message to my mother to tell her I'd arrived. I got a message back saying, "Have a wonderful weekend. Lots of love Mum xxx and Granny too x" I was perplexed by this, as my Grandmother is dead. I sent a message back asking why she had written that and got no reply. Assuming that the reception was bad I thought no more of it. When I got back home, my mother told me she had not written "and Granny too x" in the text message, and the hairs on the back of her neck had stood on end when she received my second text! I think it was just Granny making sure her presence was finally felt, in the nicest possible way.

THE NIGHTMARE LADY

Like most I look with scepticism on "ghost stories" as flights of imagination involving suggestible people. Then I remember one night when I was twelve.

Because of trouble at home (an alcoholic parent) I often stayed overnight with my Grandmother. She always rented a small house for months or sometimes several years and then moved to another. My Dad and I became experts at packing her things over the years. Our theory was that she just got tired of a place! This particular house was divided into two small apartments, leaving a bedroom in front and a kitchen and bath in each. Her neighbours were a quiet, middle-aged couple.

Granny's big bed was across the front window. Next to the bed was a large rocking chair with a footstool by it. We had gone to sleep with me next to the window. I had opened the curtains in the dark so I could look
out. It must have been about 12:30am when I was jolted fully awake by a blow across my mouth! This had the normal result of pain, confusion and terror. Revealed by the light through the window was my Grandmother sound asleep, but apparently having a nightmare! She was screaming and waving her arms in the air. Her right arm must have tagged me across the mouth.

This was a frightening sight because I'd never seen her do that before, so I rolled onto my left elbow and began shaking her shoulder to wake her. I had just started when my eyes happened to look past her to the chair beside the bed. A woman was sitting four feet from me, she was all white, sitting there with her head against the back of the chair and eyes closed. I could see every detail of her lashes and eyebrows. This wasn't possible or logical! We were alone in the apartment.

71

Being frightened by the preceding events anyway this twelve year old boy began to scream. I screamed like I meant it and I did! You are expecting the next line to be "and she vanished" aren't you?

I wish!

The Lady began to rise from the chair, but she never moved or changed position. In a sitting position with her arms seeming to be still on the chair arms and her legs straight out as if on the stool she floated into the centre of the room and I screamed louder. I saw the other furniture in the room through her and screamed louder still. The best I can describe the appearance was as if she were made of three dimensional, thin, translucent waxed paper. She seemed to be wearing some kind of nightdress which remained pressed against her bottom as if she were still sitting in the chair. In one continuous movement she described an arc across the room and her feet began disappearing through the wall into the other apartment. All this while I was still screaming and shaking my Grandmother.

The back of the woman's head was the last visible thing going into the wall. At that instant my Grandmother awoke and said, "What's wrong honey?" I couldn't speak. My mouth would not work to coherently form words. She told me I must have had a nightmare and to go back to sleep. Eventually I did.

The next day I told everyone what I'd seen. They said I was having a nightmare and would laugh at my earnest attempts to make them believe and it would move me to tears of frustration. I knew that no one could sleep through the knock that my swollen lip proved. Over the next few days I quit trying.

Three weeks later my Mother and Grandmother were staying up late in the same house reading magazines, talking and drinking coffee. Grandma went to the kitchen to make another pot of coffee when she heard someone crying. Quickly she went through the open door to the bedroom to see what was wrong with my Mother. There was nothing wrong with my mother but in the kitchen they could hear what they described as the most pitiable crying they'd ever heard. It seemed to be coming from the other apartment and was loudest beside the fridge.

The female voice would cry a while and then say "Oh Lord! Oh Danny!" They knew the couple next door wasn't home. The wife worked the second shift at a local factory and they'd heard the husband leave to bring her home. Thinking they may have a houseguest in difficulty they knocked on the front, and then the back door without success. They got a flashlight and looked all around outside.

They found no one, but they could still hear the crying from the kitchen. The crying stopped when the neighbours stepped on the porch.

They were intercepted with warnings someone was in their house, but laughed it off. They found nothing.

Grandma had paid the next month's rent only two days before, but a move was announced. She was NOT going to stay in a haunted house! While my Dad and I packed up and loaded things for an emergency move Grandma went to see the Landlady to inquire about some kind of refund on the rent. I don't remember if she got it or not, but the Landlady (who was an old friend) wanted to know why she was moving. On hearing the story she said she knew of it and that Grandma should go see a mutual friend named Bettie New and told her where she lived. On hearing the story Bettie hung her head in sadness. She had a daughter who was an alcoholic and married to a soldier. Her daughter had passed away in that house. The daughter was in a "sick" state after a long drinking binge, her husband had stayed with her as much as he could, but was out on leave and had to go back to work. On his return home he found his wife lying cold on the bathroom floor.

Betty said she had tried staying in that house herself but couldn't because "her daughter was there all the time!" One thing she was thankful for was that while her daughter was sick she had been looking after their four year old boy called Danny.

THE OLD NURSING HOME

I thought I would share just a few things with you that I have experienced over the past fourteen years working as a carer in the same nursing home in Wiltshire. The home is a very old but beautiful mansion set in large grounds and in the past not only used as a private family home but also, during the war, was used as a rehabilitation centre for the soldiers who were injured.

I have experienced many things while on duty both during the day and at night. The most common sighting from patients, passed and present is of a Lady in a Blue Dress. Many patients have mentioned her not only to me but also colleagues.

It always seems to be patients who reside in a certain corridor of the home that mention her i.e. they would ring their bell and ask whether I could make the Lady in the Blue Dress a cup of tea. What I found strange was that she was always described to us as 'the lady in the blue dress'.

Obviously I thought that this lady had to have been a passed patient of ours who resided in this part of the house and was wearing her favourite blue dress. This was until the summer almost three years ago now, I was walking along the 'haunted' corridor when I saw the sister on duty pass around the corner up some stairs. When I called out to the sister for some advice she replied from a different location. I immediately turned the corner where the person I saw vanished into thin air! I then realised that the lady in the blue dress was not an old patient of ours whatsoever but a senior nurse!

I saw her again in the same location about three months later this time she passed a doorway about two foot away from me, I knew immediately that it was her as I recognised the footwear. I can't remember hearing her or what made me look over my shoulder at the time, but there she was. On both sightings I only saw her from the waist down, not because she was headless or anything of the sort but just because of the angle I caught sight of her.

She wasn't at all what I had expected i.e. see through and ghostly but quite the opposite, she was three dimensional like you and I, she wore black tights and black lace up shoes and she walked briskly and both times vanished.

We also have mischievous ghosts which do scare me a little bit to say the least, and they get up to almost anything, again it is in certain rooms and is often dismissed by the nurses as a confused patient. It seems that some ghosts crave for attention more than others and are very persistent and let us know that it isn't the patient that is confused!

Early one evening myself and three other nurses sat taking a report from the sister when a resident rang for assistance. I answered the call, three levels up to the top of the building, I used the lift as the stairs are sometimes quite creepy. The male resident complained that his TV would not stay on one channel and kept switching through all four. I reminded him how to use his remote control and how if he pressed any of the buttons that the TV would change channels.

Happy with that I returned to the rest of the staff, two minutes later he rang again. I went again to him and he had the same complaint so I put the TV on the channel he wanted to watch and placed the remote way out of his reach on the dresser to prevent any further confusion.

He rang again and when I arrived the same old story about the TV and as I was about to leave, before my very own eyes the TV was flicking quickly through all four channels, I removed the plug told him it was faulty and legged it to the rest of the staff!

No sooner had I got down stairs to explain to the other staff the lady in the room next to him rang her bell.

This time feeling nervous I took the other three nurses with me to investigate. As we passed the man's room his door slammed shut in front of us all and as if that wasn't enough the lady in the next room who was ringing was fast asleep in her chair and her bell was about four foot away from her, on her bed!

Footsteps have also been heard late at night when everything is quiet, it is as if someone is doing a check of certain rooms. You can hear them walk then stop, then walk and stop until they reach the end of the corridor then they walk the whole length back and you can hear this most nights about two or three times.

I have saved the scariest story until last. As a night worker I am quite familiar with the goings on and confident to walk around in the dark (some nights I get a bit spooked mind you) and have been known to play a few tricks on some colleagues who are not so keen of the dark.

Now there is one place I will not go in the nursing home and that is the attic which we use as a storeroom and I believe is haunted more than any other place in the home.

One night I had to retrieve something from the attic and took a colleague (who I have previously played silly little tricks on) with me, she was nervous so I had to act the 'big brave I am'. As I entered the attic the door slammed behind me leaving me in side and her outside. She thought I had done it and I thought she had done it to teach me a lesson.

The door was locked and she was trying to tell me she couldn't unlock it, of course still thinking this was a get your own back, I thought she was pulling my leg!

I have to admit I was terrified when she began to panic and realised it wasn't her doing at all. I was stood in the corner too scared to look behind in case something was going to come and get me!

She passed the key under the door for me to try and unlock it but it just wouldn't budge. It would move freely in the lock but just wouldn't unlock! With sheer fear my colleague kicked the door open and when we tried to unlock it after, it worked just fine! This taught me a lesson and I was never a naughty girl again.

FLOATING GHOST

I would like to the share with you my tale which happened exactly twenty two years ago this very weekend.

I take myself to be a level headed sort of person, even at the tender age of thirteen years old, which I was back then. I will hold my hand up now and tell you that I am guilty of a wild and vivid imagination like a lot of people, but what befell my eyes that Sunday night has denied me any logical explanation to this very day.

I was on my way round to sit with a friend who was baby-sitting two young children. As I was early, I decided to take a walk around the houses to kill some time. I was walking through what is known as the Brownlow Fold district of Bolton, a mixture of private and local authority housing scattered around a large, and in part, derelict cotton mill.

On approaching some communal lock up type garages, I was confronted by the sight of eight to ten screaming children running from between the garages, telling me to run like hell. For what reason, I didn't know but it was soon to become frightfully apparent. I was rather puzzled by what was happening and went to investigate. To my astonishment I saw an image of a nun or monk floating some two feet off the floor appear from between the garages. It seemed to be shooing these children off as though they had disturbed it in some way. I was amazed but before I could do anything the image had disappeared and so had the children.

I think the kids where real but I am not sure about the other thing I saw.

I even went to look around these garages but could not see anything untoward. I too did not stick around for long after that either. The funny thing is I never told anybody about what I saw that night because I thought people might think I was strange. It was only years later that I decided to tell. I carried on the night with my friend who was baby-sitting but just stayed quiet. I took my leave at about 11:00pm to go home and decided to check out the area where I had spotted this image. The funny thing was I could not find it; even to this day.

GHOST WITH NO MOUTH

I moved into a house, a normal terraced house one and a half years ago and almost immediately strange things started happening. My son was two back then. I am a nurse and was on night duty one night when my husband experienced poltergeist activity.

He was sitting on the floor with a glass of juice on the glass-topped table next to him. He heard a scraping noise and turned to see the glass move in a triangle movement. It started to do it again so he put the glass on the floor as he was spooked.

Two weeks later he was out and I was lying in bed and I felt a wind whip across my face and a feeling of dread. I can't explain it but it was such an awful feeling. I later told my husband about it and this is when he told me about the glass, as he and myself are sceptics we didn't want to mention it to each other as we felt stupid.

After that we were lying in bed one night and we heard crying. Thinking it was my son I went into his bedroom and he was fast asleep so I went back to bed. A couple of seconds later our bedroom door opened then slammed shut. I ran into his bedroom thinking he was awake, but he was in exactly the same position I had just left him in and again was fast asleep.

We have noticed my son's room is always at least five degrees lower than our room. He is now recently starting to talk as kids do when they reach three years of age. He keeps saying "Black Square" is coming to get him and is genuinely frightened which in turn is frightening me. My son has said that the ghost has no mouth and wears black boots but is naughty.

Me and my husband went away for a week and my mother stayed at my house. We decided not to tell her so as not to alarm her. On our return she said our son kept going on about "Black Square".

I asked her if she had seen anything or heard anything and she told us that one night she had woken up to find a black figure standing over her. She also said she heard bangs coming from our son's room but on looking he was fast asleep.

We hear this every night now and a small child crying but can't find the root of the noise.

HAUNTINGS IN THE DALES

Back in the summer of 1993, my ex-wife and I were renting a dormer bungalow over the Bronte valley in Haworth, West Yorkshire. We were both very happy here with our one year old son but after only eighteen months we were told that we had to move out as the owners were selling. We looked around for about four weeks and eventually found an old cottage on a farmstead, it was in a very tranquil location on the edge of the Yorkshire Dales.

The building itself dated back to the thirteenth century and was originally used as a threshing barn but was made habitable in the 19th century. Not long after moving our relationship gradually changed and we became very distant. I had an office at home and once a week I would work from the office in the spare room upstairs, my wife would take our son over to her mothers to leave me in peace to work.

At around 10:30am I would go downstairs to make a coffee and without fail would find the TV switched on. I would constantly remind my wife to turn it off and she would insist she had. One morning I had started working upstairs as usual and could clearly hear voices, thinking the TV had been left on as usual I went to investigate but when I stepped off the bottom step the voices stopped and I realised the TV was in fact turned off.

A couple of years passed with the odd strange happening but nothing that couldn't be explained away. I was now living there on my own after seperating from my wife, most nights whilst laid in bed I would hear voices downstairs but would never dare investigate.

One night I was collecting coal from the bunker across the farmyard when the hairs on the back of my neck suddenly stood on end and even though it was quite mild outside. I felt a chill to my bones I started to feel like someone was staring at me so I turned to look back and froze to the spot. About four feet away on the other side of the farm gate was a dark shadowy outline of a very tall man which slowly faded away. I never collected the coal in the dark again after that night.

The living room had been enlarged before we moved there. Originally there had been a walk-in pantry which had been taken out to extend the living room. On the floor of the pantry there had been an old oak trap door leading to a cellar. The cellar had been filled with hardcore as it was felt the stone slab floor had become unsafe. I would sit watching TV most nights and would suddenly feel and hear three or four loud thuds coming from what would have been the cellar.

One night, directly following these noises I looked up to see a young man looking through the window. Immediately I realised that what I was actually seeing was the reflection of someone stood behind looking down at me! I turned sharply to find no one there. This really had a very bad affect on me and I became very nervy and always on the edge finding it very difficult to sleep. I confided in my sister what I had seen but didn't feel comfortable telling anyone else for fear of ridicule.
I will never forget the old cottage or my experiences there, the one thing it has given me is a very strong hunger for any thing paranormal and I, like many others, want to learn more.

GHOSTS IN THE MACHINE

Two years ago I bought what was then a state of the art computer from a local computer store. Within two days of having the machine installed in our home strange and bizarre things started happening.

The room where the computer was installed was always cold, easily ten to fifteen degrees colder than the rest of the house. At first I thought there was a draft in the room, but we moved the computer into our 'living' room and within three days the temperature drop started happening in there.

The computer was then put back into its original location. As a computer freak I started buying add-ons, you know scanner printer and such like, but whenever we tried using them, they refused point blank to work. Computer programs would vanish (I don't mean data crashes) pictures would alter themselves, internet connection wouldn't work, phone line started going nuts (at this point the home telephone would be back to normal as soon as the computer was unplugged from the phone socket).

At first I thought that the machine was faulty. Engineers came and looked at it, and everything was fine. My sister refused to go anywhere near the machine and seven year old kids love computers!

Worse was to come, the lights in the computer room would start turning themselves off and on. Then strange smells started to appear, I couldn't smell these but my mum could. Strange text was appearing on the screen, some was gobbledegook, some were things like "leave me alone". Stains were starting to appear on the machines casing.

It was truly freaky, but the last thing that prompted us to get rid of the machine was a scary experience. We started seeing shadows always by the machine and getting feelings of nervousness, the family dog refused point blank to enter the room, and worse of all a smell of burning filled the room. So, we decided to let my elder brother borrow the thing. The room temperature returned to normal and all the feelings had gone.

He has never had anything happen to him regarding the machine and he knew what was going on even before he borrowed it, maybe the machine or whatever 'lives' inside it preferred him to us.

HAUNTED HARROGATE HOUSE

My family live in a house that was originally built alongside the train-tracks in Harrogate, once it was home to several families. During the first and second World Wars the house became a refuge for children who travelled from neighbouring cities to escape the raids.

The woman who looked after these children was born in the house and from what I have heard never had children of her own. The house was apparently a haven for children, and this woman dedicated her life to looking after them.

In circa 1960, my Father bought the house whereupon his Mother (a medium who used to hold regular séances in the town hall) rushed to the top of the stairs and proclaimed there was a little girl sat next to her! Not only that but the girl would look after my Father's children in the future and this was twenty-one years before my sister and I were born.

There are countless stories of events taking place while he lived there as a bachelor, from objects moving around, to lights going on and off, the sound of footsteps and so forth. However, there was no feeling of harm or evil in the house. The house was always very welcoming.

When my sister and I lived there between the ages of nine and twelve, there were plenty of events I can remember, most of which still frighten me to this day.
Saying that however, nothing bad ever happened in the house, we were never hurt nor bothered. I remember scientists coming round to the house once, and they set up equipment at the bottom of the stairs pointing up.

I remember this being a great playground story at school. Apparently there were recordings made, though I never saw them myself.

I did see this sprit once however, standing behind my Father was a little girl in a polka-dot dress waving at me and my friends. I remember trying to shout at my Dad to turn around but nothing came out of my mouth.

I was speechless and my two friends at the time ran away in tears. I often saw tennis balls and ping-pong balls bouncing down the stairs, and when this did happen I would run to the living room and hide. As a child it was extremely disturbing.

GHOST ATTACK OR NIGHTMARE?

Last August I went on my first all lads holiday to Ibiza.

After five nights of excessive drinking, me and one of my friends opted to stay in on our second last night, and recover for our last night on the island.

It was twenty-four hours since my previous alcoholic drink, so any speculation of still being drunk was most definitely not an option. Anyway, after sleeping comfortably for a few hours I woke up to a movement by the door.

The room was extremely dark and only a strong shadow or reflection could have been identified. I then saw what I thought was my friend kneeling on my bed leaning over my sleeping mate to the right of me.

I saw the shadowed reflection move across the bed in the same motion as a man would move, who was crawling over two people in a double bed, if you can imagine.

By this time I was frozen on my bed feet away from this mysterious intruder. I screamed at the top of my voice the name of my mate who I thought had just returned from the night out, trying to creep in on me.

I then tried my hardest to kick the intruder as if to say to my mate cut it out. However, my leg was completely frozen and I couldn't lift it off the bed, furthermore my voice was still silent. Only my eyes were moving following this figure. Then the shadow stopped over me on all fours. By this time I was scared, not knowing what was happening, and when I opened my eyes a second later the shadowed intruder had gone. I felt a presence draw my eyes to the locked balcony doors where I remember to this day, the curtains shook for a second and my conscious nightmare disappeared, and my body became free from the state in which I encountered.

I've been told I suffered a night paralysis or sleep psychosis, which means my body was still in a deep sleep and my brain was vibrant and very much awake. But that still leaves me thinking, I know what I saw, and I definitely was not asleep.

THE SCHOOL'S GHOSTS

I work in a large secondary school in South Yorkshire, and live in a bungalow on the site. Over the past five years or so there have been a few strange occurrences, both in the school and in my bungalow.

The first 'event' happened when my eldest son worked in a bakery about two miles away. He had started work a 6:00am on that day, and I was starting at 8:15am. I was just about to get up at 7:30am when I heard the back door open and heavy footsteps across the floor, his bedroom door opened and closed, and a couple of minutes later the bedroom door opened and shut again. Then I heard more footsteps across the floor and then out of the back door. I didn't think anything about it, he's a big lad and I assumed he'd forgotten his money or something. However, when he came home and I asked him what he'd forgotten, he hadn't been home. The strange thing was, the back door was locked and the dog was asleep in the kitchen and never made a sound.

Two years ago in November, I was in the school at 5:30pm when I saw a young lad aged about twelve or thirteen walk across the next room through the glass panel next to the door. He was wearing a blue jacket and had yellow blonde hair in a kind of 'curtains' style that was popular in the nineties. I gave him a couple of minutes to come back, as he shouldn't have been in school at that time. When I went to look for him, I bumped into the caretaker who came from the place where the lad was heading and he hadn't seen anybody, neither had the cleaners who were working in the block. Interestingly, I was locking up in that same room some months later when a door which I had just closed opened and shut again. We also have a photograph taken by some pupils last Easter which clearly shows a woman sitting in a chair in that room. She wasn't visible to anyone when the picture was taken.

Finally, (for now) early in 2006 I was walking across the playground at 11:35am one Saturday morning, I saw a man on the field in front of me. We have a security fence, and I wondered how he had got in. He appeared to be playing golf, as I saw him bend down as if he was placing a ball on a tee. He was middle aged, with short hair that was dark going grey, he was wearing what looked like a light grey sweatshirt. I could only see him from the knees up, but didn't think anything about it because the field is at a level of about eight feet above the yard where I was. I set off to ask him what he was doing on school property. While I was making my way there I lost sight of him for a moment. I reached the top of the banking and disturbed a large flock of seagulls which were sitting on the exact spot where I'd seen the man. If there had been anyone 'real' there the seagulls would have been disturbed by him. I looked round the field but there was nobody in sight.

Other caretakers have heard footsteps, music that stops when they look to see where it's coming from and lots of weird things. I dare not give the name of the school unfortunately.

GLASGOW HAUNTINGS

For as long as I can remember, there has always been ghosts around me. When I was around ten years old I lived with my parents and six siblings in a two bedroom tenement block in Glasgow.

I had been out playing with friends and forgetting the time it had turned dark, I made my way the short distance from my friends home to my own. On getting home I found out that my younger sister with whom I shared a bed with, was spending the night at a friends house. I decided that I wanted to sleep in the living room, and being that we lived on the ground floor we were always careful to lock all the windows and doors at night. On this particular night I was awoken with a strong cool breeze and as I opened my eyes there was a horseman dressed in white standing over me with a raised sword! I screamed like you wouldn't believe, and when my family came running to the living room the lights wouldn't switch on and the windows were opened fully!

A few days later in the local newspaper there had been reported sightings of a white horseman on a white horse, after this experience I was totally traumatised and could not sleep without a light on for around four years.

We then moved to a larger house and after a few months I would get the feeling that I was being watched, it was as if there was always someone right behind me. In the room that I shared with my younger sister occasionally the shadow of a figure that would rock back and forth was seen on the bedroom wall. It was as if someone was in a rocking chair but no chair or figure was there!

Sometimes I would be woken at night with the weight of someone sitting on the edge of my bed, but there was nothing to be seen. One night my younger sister had gone to bed early as she had the flu, she awoke in the morning and asked who had tucked her into bed so tightly? She complained that she could barely move as the covers were so tight but no one had done it!

We began to have a bit of bad luck health wise in our home and we lost three members of our family, two within two weeks of each other. By this time there was only myself, my son, my sister, brother, niece and a neighbour who worked for a priest at this time. I told him all about our loss and he told us "get those girls out of that house!" So my sister, niece and brother moved out a short time after leaving just my son and I.

I then met my partner and he moved in with us, on one occasion when I had a big argument with him I told him to pack and go and I left for work. He showed up later on and told me as he was packing he had been going about it in a rage and there were flashes of light shooting up and down the living room. I have never seen him look so scared.

We moved again to a house that I could finally call my own, since we've been here I have always felt a presence in the house, but never felt scared.
We often smell cigarettes when walking around upstairs, both my son and his girlfriend don't smoke and have no reason to hide it. Another time my son's girlfriend had been downstairs in the bathroom and asked my son who the old lady was, when he asked her what she was talking about she said an old lady passed her in the hall.

I myself on a couple of occasions have seen a figure on the top landing, but it seems to be centered around my son's bedroom. There was one night we were awoken with an almighty crashing of glass being broken, thinking we were being burgled my son, partner and myself all raced down stairs to find nothing!

This week my son again, came into my room around four in the morning quite visibly shaken and asked if id been up

94

using the bathroom? I told him I hadn't, which he replied, "then I've just been talking to a ghost!" He went on to explain that he was just about to go to the bathroom when he heard the bathroom light switch on, he then heard footsteps coming upstairs. Thinking it was me going back to bed he came out of his bedroom which is next door to mine, and saw a small figure and said "Oh I got a fright there" thinking it was me. He then came back up stairs and saw the figure again, then it disappeared!

THE MYSTERY LADY

I am sure this will be dismissed as total fiction, but I promise it is true.

When I was eighteen I had a girlfriend who lived twenty miles away at Park Gate, Southampton. To get to, and from there I regularly used the train from Cosham to Swanwick station. To get home on this particular SUNDAY evening, I arrived at 11:00pm on Swanwick station. It is a fairly remote and dingy station and it was unusual for anybody else to be there at this hour, but a lady in her late 40's or early 50's was seated waiting for the last train.

She was about 5ft 4 inches tall, of plump build, with permed hair, and was wearing a "camel" coat and was carrying a very large canvas shopping bag, which had a tartan pattern on.

I sat down to wait for the train (which were frequently late). After a few minutes the lady asked if there was a train as she "had to get back to Portsmouth". I told her that I was also waiting for the same train and that it should be along soon.

Several times she asked the same question and reinforced that she "must get back to Portsmouth". When the train eventually did arrive, she remained seated but became very agitated and began to cry. I told her that this was the last train, but several times between sobs she repeated "I can't go back". I asked if I could help, and suggested that if she got on the train that perhaps we could talk about any problems she had. But again she said, "I can't go back."

Meanwhile the guard had got off of the train to point out that this was the last train of the night and that if I was getting on I should hurry (from his angle he probably couldn't see the lady). Reluctantly I got on the train, and as it pulled out of the station I could see her sobbing.

On the journey home I felt guilty about leaving her, as she was obviously very upset about something. On arriving home at Cosham I telephoned the Police at Park Gate and briefly related the story and asked if perhaps somebody could visit the railway station and see if she was ok. I gave a description of her height, dress, and the bag she was carrying. I assumed that perhaps some domestic dispute was the cause of her distress.

On arriving home from work the next evening (Monday) my mother drew my attention to an article in the local paper, "The Evening News". She knew that I caught the train from Swanwick and this article was appealing for witnesses to an accident near that station. I immediately recognised the photograph included in the article as the lady from the previous evening, the description of her clothing, height, dress and bag also matched perfectly.

The article was appealing for witnesses to an accident where the lady had been killed whilst walking along the railway lines.... ON THE SATURDAY EVENING. I telephoned the newspaper and suggested that they had confused the dates, and that I had spoken to the lady, they checked and to my surprise insisted that the accident had been on SATURDAY. I then telephoned the police who listened to my story, and indeed confirmed that I had reported the incident on SUNDAY evening, however were adamant that the incident had occurred on the SATURDAY.

In a subsequent article in the local paper I learned that the lady was called Maureen Hampton, she was a patient in a local mental hospital (Coldeast). She had been allowed out on the Saturday and had been to Portsmouth. Returning in the evening, she had missed the station at Swanwick and got off of the train at the next stop (Bursledon), not being familiar with the area she had decided to walk the short distance back to Swanwick along the lines, and was struck by a train.

Now, I wish I had remained or touched her! However, I caught the bus after this!

A30 GHOST

I am going back a few years now but I encountered a ghostly sighting on the A30 west bound to Cornwall.

I was driving along on my way to visit friends who live in Cornwall, I was aware of a small yellow van that had appeared from nowhere. I carried on driving whilst keeping my eye on it in the rear view mirror, the van was not getting any closer to me.

This happened for a few miles and I had still not passed any exits of the A30. I then looked in my rear view mirror again and it had just disappeared. This now really freaked me out!

To this day I cannot find an answer to this encounter as I have driven down the same road as I still do today, and there are no turn off's from where I saw this small yellow van. This was not just down to seeing or thinking I was seeing it because of the distance travelled with the van in my sights, so I believe the A30 or parts of it to be haunted.

A GHOST IN SUFFOLK

I recently purchased a property in a very small village / rural hamlet. This property has a large garden that backs onto what was once, some forty years back I believe, an old railway track.

Fully overgrown with many sections now sold off, it only vaguely resembles an old track. One evening I was out in the pitch black doing a bonfire and removing the garden of all brambles etc. The evening was somewhat fresh and I did feel a sudden coldness, even though the fire was taking very nicely.

I thought nothing of it until some ten minutes later I saw in amongst the over grown track a blue shaded figure move along approximately five metres. Again, no alarm bells as folk from the village no doubt walk dogs etc at night.

I then realised the figure had disappeared and re-appeared where it started and repeated it's approximate five metre walk. I honestly darted for the house and since then I am very reluctant at night to venture to the area at the bottom of the garden.

I have researched online, but found no reference to any weird sightings locally, nearest supposed ghost sightings were at 'The Bull Inn', Long Melford, Suffolk.

I haven't had the confidence to ask any neighbours simply because we have just moved in and its not exactly everyday conversation. I don't want to mention it too much either, in case if affects value of house if that makes sense, cause we are in the process of modernising it with a view to remarketing it.

A PUB WITH SPIRITS

One summer day in 1987 myself and two friends happened to have the same weekday off work and so decided to visit some record shops in London.

We traipsed around half the day buying records and clothes etc and then decided to stop for a rest and a beer. At this time I was working and living in a private psychiatric clinic on Harrow-on-the-Hill. The staff accommodation was situated at the very top of the old building away from the residents and with restricted access through locked doors.

Myself and a colleague who also lived there were experiencing unusual events such as movement of items in our rooms, I once came in to find a perfect circle of glass marbles on the floor. Other things happened such as TVs turned on when we were out, chairs moving and the piano in the lounge playing with no one in the room.

Anyway, my friends and I walked into a pub called 'Ye Olde Swiss Cottage' on the Finchley Road in London for a rest. It was the first time any of us had been there although we had passed it on many occasions. It is a large pub designed like a Swiss chalet on the outside and inside has low-beamed ceilings and is spacious.

At the back of the bar we could see a few pool tables with a couple of games going on. Apart from the people playing pool the bar was empty. We sat down at the bar and waited for the barman to come out from the back to serve us. As we were waiting I was telling my friends about the strange things that were happening at the place where I was living. When the barman came we started chatting to him. He was from New Zealand and friendly.

As we were talking I heard heavy footsteps on the ceiling above. I noticed the barman look up and raise his eyebrows.

So, jokingly I said to him, "What's the noise, a ghost?" He quite seriously said, "yes" and began to tell us that he lived in on the job with a few others and often had problems sleeping due to strange things happening in the night.

He then went away and I carried on talking to my friends, carrying on the previous topic of conversation as before. Suddenly, we all stopped talking as we heard a high-pitched sound like a ping or cracking sound. It was so loud it made all three of us stop in our tracks. Looking around we noticed that the thick, heavy, green glass ashtray on the bar was in two pieces with a perfectly clean break down the middle. The ashtray was clean and unused as none of us was smoking.

I thought it may have just come out of a dishwasher but it was not even warm. We were shocked and mystified so we called the barman. He just let out a long sigh looked at it for a few seconds and replaced it with a new one.

We felt uncomfortable after that but stayed a little longer out of curiosity. Sorry to say nothing else happened but we were sure we'd upset the resident ghost by the topic of our discussion and she or he wanted to let us know we were being watched. We certainly felt it. I've had other unexplained experiences in my life but nothing for about ten years now.

MY EXPERIENCES OF WINGATES GROVE

The following is a witness experience of a notoriously haunted estate in Bolton by the name of Wingates Grove. For nearly twenty years there have been continual reports of paranormal activity.

I wanted to tell you that I became a tenant of a house on Wingates Grove. On accepting the house I was told by the housing officer that there had been some reported activity by previous tenants, I called the Spiritualist Association prior to accepting and was quite happy with their response.

I decided to say nothing to any one about the information given to me. However whilst decorating the house both my friend (total sceptic) and my ex-husband (policeman and most unimaginative person on the planet) both heard footsteps on the bare stairs and reported that items moved from where they had been left. At this point we all agreed to say nothing to the children and see what happened.

Things disappeared and reappeared on a regular basis, keys went missing and would be found later in places that had been searched or often in the middle of a room on the floor.

The pets were quite happy and didn't appear to be bothered by whatever it was, at this point I had still not said anything to the kids and told them it was nonsense when the neighbours kids told them the house was haunted.
The pets would often seem to watch as if someone was walking through the room and the dog would often lie on her back as if her belly was being petted. It was only when my daughter started telling me she could see animals in her room and she had seen a shape standing at the foot of her bed and felt uneasy.

Things started turning themselves on and off, TV channels changed, volume went up and down, the smoke alarm went off in the night.

We called our guest Oscar and talked to him. I left the house with a house sitter when I took the kids away and upon our return the guy who had been in the house told me I should have told him the house was haunted! He had seen the ghost one evening and it had scared him. He couldn't understand why things kept moving.

Recently the council were to do some work on the house and I had several visits from the housing office and contractors about the house and I agreed that they could bring in someone to pray for whatever was here.

Two very pleasant lady vicars came and said prayers. It was explained that everything should be fine now but if not the next step was a mass in the house. I again told the kids that the house is fine now and so far they have not reported anything.

MY NEIGHBOUR RETURNED

I have a story to tell you that may be of great interest to you. When I was fourteen, a friend and I went into Belgrave Hall which is supposedly haunted. We were just kids messing about. In one of the rooms I hopped over the barrier to pinch a little plastic egg off the kitchen table. The alarms went off and the museum owner was called but we was let off with a warning.

That night I went to bed as usual with my two brothers who share a room with me. I fell asleep thinking nothing of the day's events. I woke in the night and the bedroom door was closed, cutting off the light from the bathroom. My quilt had slipped to the floor and as I pulled it across me I couldn't help notice a figure moving towards me. A dark figure with a recognisable face to me, I could see it was someone I knew - my next door neighbour from years before. He was an old man who had lost most of his teeth. He had his fangs though, just like he did in life, which made him look like a vampire.

I hid under the quilt and lay there petrified all night, waiting to hear either my Mum or Dad get up. The bed was wet through from sweating all night. I couldn't even bring myself to shout them, I don't think I've ever been so afraid. Because of that paranormal experience, I have always believed in ghosts. Now over twenty years on, I don't fear ghosts at all. I turn lights out in the hope of one coming to me again. Should it ever happen again I wouldn't be afraid at all.

OLD COUPLE RETURNS

To be honest, most of my life I've had luck or bad luck, depending on how you view it, of being surrounded by paranormal activity. Only in the last few years have I started to really study the paranormal in depth, and I find that the more I learn, the more I want to dig deeper into it. The following is about one of many experiences I've had.

Years ago, my family and I had moved into a house, an old one that had been remodelled several times. It was a large home, my two sisters and I were thrilled as we would finally have our own rooms. Our parents seemed to have finally found a beautiful home. It seemed bright and cheerful, had almost an acre of land, and was just far enough from the city to be quiet.

About a month after moving in, we would start to hear someone walking upstairs. At first we thought this was due to the house settling, after all, it was old. On occasion you would catch a flash of something darting from the corner of your eye which looked like a dark shadow. Sometimes small, the size of a dog, other times a larger one. Our cat called Shadow would follow and watch things that we couldn't see. My dad pretty much shrugged all of it off. My mum, sisters, and myself found it exciting, we had yet again moved into a home with ghosts.

As the first year progressed, so did the activity. One of my sisters had two big walk-in closets in her room, each having a light. No matter how many times we closed the doors and turned the lights out, a few minutes later when we checked, the lights were on and the doors wide open. Off the living room were two other rooms. One was an extra bedroom (my parent's) and the other was once a porch, now closed in and with a small bathroom. Once in a while, you would be sitting in the living room or the dining room, and hear the voice of what sounded like a man yelling, "Hey!" What I found curious was that there was no bad feeling in our house, it was like we were just sharing a house with an 'invisible' roommate.

The man who owned the house came by one day to talk to my dad about something, and we asked him about the history of the house. We did not mention any of the activity that was happening. The original owners were an elderly couple, they had lived in the house for decades and the man died in the house. Since then the house had been on and off the market for years, and we had an idea why.

Over the next few years, we became used to the activity. My mother had one experience where she was in the kitchen, she happened to glance down the hallway, to where the landing of the stairs were. For a moment a shadowy figure of a woman was standing there and slowly disappeared. Our cat had a hatred for the back bedroom off the closed in porch. You couldn't drag him back there, all he would do was stand at a safe distance, hunching up and hissing.

We also had two very entertaining occurrences happen. Once we were having dinner in the dining room, and we kept hearing an odd noise. It sounded familiar but we couldn't figure out what it was so my youngest sister and I went to see what it was. When we got into the living room we happened to look over by the entrance that let on into the hallway. Our phone, an old rotary, was dialling itself. We stood there speechless, then ran back and told everyone what it was. By this time, even my dad had experienced a few odd things, he did not want to go to see the phone dial.

The other occurrence happened one evening while we were all in the living room watching a movie. We had heard a few noises in the kitchen, but didn't think too much of them. By now we would chalk it up to the old woman, who seemed to be the practical joker of the ghosts.

We then heard something, and went into the kitchen. To this day, I can't explain it. Something had locked the dishwasher, and started it. There had been no one in the kitchen, and the dishwasher door was slid over to the unlocked position. My mother did not sleep well that night!

We ended up moving after living there for about five years due to a job change for my dad. I found myself a bit sad that we wouldn't have our 'old couple' to keep us company. I thought that maybe they would possibly follow us, this had happened before, but they didn't. I guess they really loved their old home, and probably still do today.

THE GHOST CAR

My husband and myself now both retired love to go on leisure drives. One cool but bright afternoon we decided to go out, around lunchtime. We don't like to use main highways so mostly we use country lanes so with my two daughters sitting in the back off we went.

We were driving along an old roman road in our area at the back of Weston Park in Sheffield and the road ran straight as a bullet in both directions apart from the slight dips. We were the only car on the road.

Suddenly out of the passenger wing mirror I saw a large dark car coming after us really fast! I watched it rising up and down the dips in the road and noticed my husband spot it in his mirror. I felt him adjust the car's speed and move over slightly to let him pass when he reached us.

Then I noticed there was something weird about the shape of the car. To me it looked like a very old Wolsey with large round front bumpers, a car I had not seen on the road for decades. It came up right behind us then moved out my view as if to overtake. My hubby slowed right down and pulled to the side as far as he could get to let him pass, then I saw the car pulling alongside. The car came past where my daughters were sitting then came level with my husband's window. I looked and saw what I took to be a man hunched over the wheel, only one occupant, and the wheel was large but I couldn't see a face.

As it drew level it suddenly vanished! I said to my husband where did he go and my hubby shouted, "did you see that? Did you see that?"

I thought I imagined it, I said I've been watching him come from about a good mile and a half back. When we asked our two daughters if they had seen him neither of them had.

For a long time after we told no one about this, thinking people would think us mad. It was a bright sunny afternoon at about 1:00pm, was this a ghost? We can't explain it to this day, can you?

SAFFRON MALDON MOOT HALL

In my home town of Maldon is a place called the Moot Hall. It was built in the 1100's and has acted as the town's police station, gaol, court house and council offices, as a matter of fact; the word 'Moot' is derived from a Saxon word meaning place of Meeting. It is a three storied building, on the ground floor is the old police station and cells, and prisoner's courtyard, the first floor is home to the old court room and the second floor is the council meeting room and old Mayor's Parlour.

I first visited this place about a year ago and got talking to the guide (there are two tours held in the building on Saturday afternoons in the summer months). I asked her casually if there was any history of paranormal disturbance within the building, she then went on to tell me of her own experiences. She claimed to have seen several dark shadowy figures go across the room in the old police station on the ground floor. She also hears things being moved around upstairs in the building when there can't possibly be anyone inside at the time. She used to open up for tours and find doors opened that had been closed the previous night, find furniture moved around and other strange experiences like this. In terms of veridical evidence, there have been several photos taken at the location showing orbs and mist, and even on one occasion a photo taken in the prisoners courtyard showed the faint outline of a person stood in a corner.

I have paid several visits to this location over the last year and have had various experiences involving audible phenomena such as, on one occasion while speaking to the guide in the downstairs police station. Two other witnesses and I heard the sound of a door being slammed shut on one of the upper floors. At that point in time the door that accessed the upper floors was shut and locked. The only way to these upper floors is through an external door. We promptly moved to the upper floors to find the cause of these noises, only to find no change to the doors, which had all been closed when the guide was last in that area. This suggests to me two actual occurrences had taken place, one being the original opening of the door which we later heard slammed, remember that we would not have heard the door being opened in the first place as it would not have caused sufficient noise.

One another occasion during a tour that contained another eight people at least, while all group members were in the Mayor's parlour, we heard the sound of a chair being dragged across the floor. The sound was very brief, lasting only a few seconds, but very distinct. I immediately checked all chairs and carried out a baseline test of the room, no anomalous results were picked up on the test. The other members of the tour can all verify that this event had taken place as it resulted in me asking them many questions.

I am still investigating this place and have as yet to reach a conclusion.

THE GHOST OF THE HALIFAX BOMBER

About six years ago I was visiting my parents in Market Harborough Leicestershire. They live quite near the Imperial War Museum at Duxford and on summer afternoons Spitfires and Mustangs are a common sight flying over their back garden.

About 3:00pm on a Sunday afternoon a Handley-Page "Halifax" four engined World War II bomber flew overhead. I'm a bit of a plane nerd and it was clearly a Halifax not a Lancaster (it had triangular tail fins, radial engines, no nose turret and squared off wing tips). More importantly than my identification my parent's neighbour who flew liberator bombers for coastal command also saw it and said, "bloody hell - a Halifax!" He's a very sharp eighty year old and as an ex-bomber pilot knows his World War II aircraft.

The odd thing is that there are no complete Halifaxes in museums (three exist but they're built from bits or wrecks). There are apparently no airworthy ones and I've been unable to find any record of replicas or conversions that could have fooled us. There was a civilian freighter version (the Halton) made after the war and I've considered that someone could have converted one back to look like a WW2 bomber, but no Haltons are listed as surviving never mind flying and you'd expect such a plane to be a big feature at air shows.

The plane was flying fast overhead South to North at about thousand feet. We both heard it and it behaved exactly like you would expect a real plane to behave. I'd estimate we watched it for about forty five seconds before it was obscured by the houses in the next street. It certainly wasn't a reflection, projection or anything else. The plane was in good condition (it wasn't on fire or battle damaged) but looked more 'real' than many restored to flying condition with matt paint rather than a glossy finish.

I'd be really grateful if you could provide any explanation for this as its been driving me crazy ever since!

OUIJA BOARD EXPERIENCE

Just before I tell my tale you may not believe it, I'm not even sure if I believe it but I promise I am not lying.

In the early days of June this year my friend had what seemed safe idea of doing an Ouija board. The first time we did it we decided that we would circulate our fingers on the glass enabling our self to push it. That particular group of friends I had only recently befriended and did not know much of each other's past. The first spirit that visited us was a young man called 'Bob Cutter'. We asked him about himself. His background seemed a bit cliché since he was murdered and so on. He left after about ten minutes so we decided to do it again.

Quite quickly a spirit made it clear that they were present. We asked the spirits first name and it said 'Doug' then we asked its second name and it said 'Field'. While communicating with Doug Field everything seemed very cold and the glass moved on its own accord.

Suddenly my friend who was sat in the corner burst into tear shouting "stop please stop" so we quickly took our fingers off the glass and went to comfort her. She told us that her deceased grandfather was called 'Doug Field'!

We cleared away the Ouija board and burnt it. My friend told her mother of the event and the mother said that her grandfather's death day was in two weeks time.

HAUNTINGS AT KENTISH TOWN

I have had some weird things happen to me over the years.

The first being when I was seventeen years old, I used to stay with a friend in Kentish town, London. She lives in an old house and when going up the stairs to the bedrooms, I always felt I had to run up the last few stairs, feeling like someone was above or behind me. We informed the landlord of my feelings and she told us about a young boy who had hang himself at that point on the staircase.

Another strange time that happened was in an ex-partner's house also in Kentish town. He lived in a basement flat of an old house and from the very first time I stayed there, I knew the house was haunted.

On the first night I had a nightmare that there were three people standing at the end of my bed watching me. I woke up scared and thought I could still see them there. This happened most times I stayed there.

Sometimes when I walked into the kitchen I would see in the corner of my eye that a tall shadow of a man was walking into the bathroom. I told my ex-boyfriend how I was feeling to which he admitted he seen the same thing!

One night I was lying in bed when I saw what looked like a young girl and what seemed to be a large man sitting in the chair! We decided to try and find information on this flat and we discovered that a man in a wheelchair had died in the hallway, which is where the bedroom door is situation.

Everything seemed to calm down after we heard about the man who died, but things kicked off again after my boyfriend painted the bathroom white. Just after painting the bathroom he noticed what looked like several small child's handprints appearing in the paint. Strangely they appeared high up on the wall and not low down!

We have since separated and as far as I know he still lives there, I never felt comfortable in his flat and will never return.

From the Author

I hope you enjoyed my first collection of original ghost experiences and the vast array of phenomena reported by the witnesses. If you would like to submit an experience or was a witness to some of the stories in this book please email mj@mjwayland.com

Also for further ghost stories and research as well as my future releases please visit my website - www.mjwayland.com

Thank you

MJ Wayland

My other books include:

50 Real Ghost Stories 2
Real Christmas Ghost Stories
The York Ghost Walk
The Derby Ghost Walk
Tales of the Polden Hills

All are available from Amazon and other good bookshops.

Printed in Poland
by Amazon Fulfillment
Poland Sp. z o.o., Wrocław